STUDIES IN AFRICAN HISTORY

Volume 3

I0127902

MILITARY RÉGIMES
IN AFRICA

MILITARY RÉGIMES
IN AFRICA

W. F. GUTTERIDGE

Routledge
Taylor & Francis Group
LONDON AND NEW YORK

First published in 1975 by Methuen & Co. Ltd.

This edition first published in 2024
by Routledge
4 Park Square, Milton Park, Abingdon, Oxon OX14 4RN

and by Routledge
605 Third Avenue, New York, NY 10158

Routledge is an imprint of the Taylor & Francis Group, an informa business

British Library Cataloguing in Publication Data
A catalogue record for this book is available from the British Library

ISBN: 978-1-032-62258-3 (Set)
ISBN: 978-1-032-61281-2 (Volume 3) (hbk)
ISBN: 978-1-032-61300-0 (Volume 3) (pbk)
ISBN: 978-1-003-46288-0 (Volume 3) (ebk)

DOI: 10.4324/9781003462880

Publisher's Note
The publisher has gone to great lengths to ensure the quality of this reprint but points out that some imperfections in the original copies may be apparent.

Disclaimer
The publisher has made every effort to trace copyright holders and would welcome correspondence from those they have been unable to trace.

W. F. GUTTERIDGE

MILITARY RÉGIMES
IN AFRICA

METHUEN & CO LTD
11 New Fetter Lane · London EC4

First published 1975 by Methuen & Co Ltd
Reprinted 1976
© *1975 W. F. Gutteridge*
Printed in Great Britain by
Butler & Tanner Ltd
Frome and London

ISBN 416 78230 2   hardback
ISBN 416 78240 X   paperback

Distributed in the USA
by HARPER & ROW PUBLISHERS, INC.
BARNES & NOBLE IMPORT DIVISION

Contents

Preface

My previous book in this series, *The Military in African Politics* (1969), was primarily concerned with the inherited characteristics of the African military and the causes and incidence of coups. When the time came to consider its revision for a possible second edition, five years later, it seemed more appropriate to write a sequel which would, as it were, take up the threads of the first work and at the same time concern itself more with performance in power than with the seizure of it. Such has been the advance in the study of the military in Africa, made possible by a decade of coups. Each of the six cases selected seemed in a special way significant, if only because it tended to emphasize the unique nature of the particular situation. In order to avoid repetition and excessive involvement with the trivia of history, three of the cases have been treated at some length and the remainder in such a way as to bring out what I perceive in the light of the first three to be their essential characteristics.

I am grateful to the General Editor, A. H. M. Kirk-Greene, for his encouragement and to those in daily contact with me at home and at work for their help and tolerance while I have been engaged on the book.

University of Aston, Birmingham, 1974

WILLIAM GUTTERIDGE

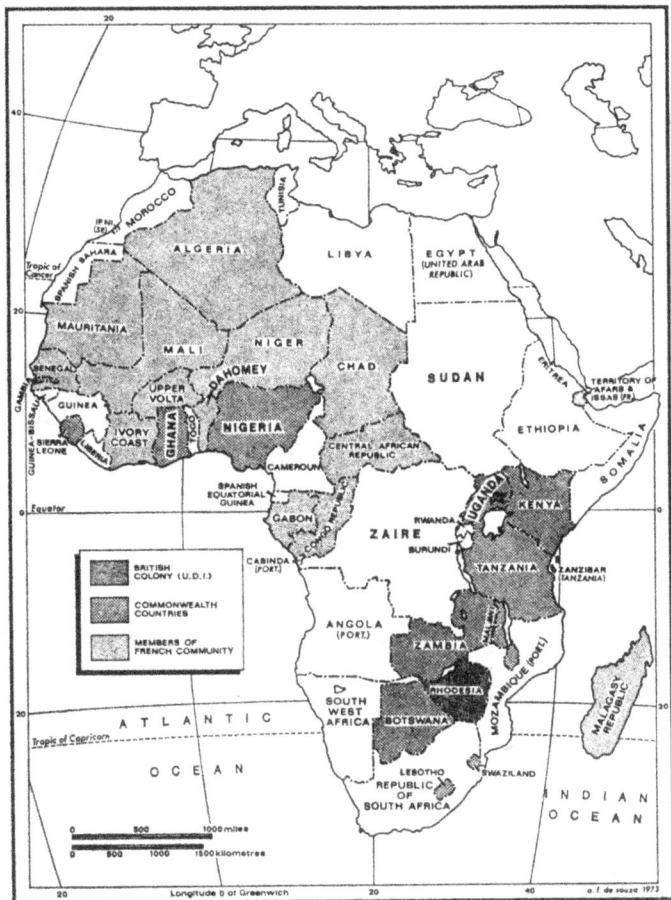

MOROCCO
IFNI (SP.)
SPANISH SAHARA
TUNISIA
ALGERIA
LIBYA
EGYPT (UNITED ARAB REPUBLIC)
Tropic of Cancer
20
MAURITANIA
MALI
NIGER
CHAD
SUDAN
ERITREA
TERRITORY OF AFARS & ISSAS (FR.)
SENEGAL
GAMBIA
GUINEA-BISSAU
GUINEA
SIERRA LEONE
IVORY COAST
UPPER VOLTA
GHANA
TOGO
DAHOMEY
NIGERIA
CAMEROUN
CENTRAL AFRICAN REPUBLIC
ETHIOPIA
SOMALIA
SPANISH EQUATORIAL GUINEA
GABON
CONGO
ZAIRE
RWANDA
BURUNDI
UGANDA
KENYA
Equator
0
TANZANIA
ZANZIBAR (TANZANIA)
CABINDA (PORT.)
ANGOLA (PORT.)
ZAMBIA
MALAWI
MOZAMBIQUE (PORT.)
RHODESIA
BOTSWANA
MALAGASY REPUBLIC
SOUTH WEST AFRICA
ATLANTIC
OCEAN
20
Tropic of Capricorn
LESOTHO
REPUBLIC OF SOUTH AFRICA
SWAZILAND
INDIAN
OCEAN

BRITISH COLONY (U.D.I.)

COMMONWEALTH COUNTRIES

MEMBERS OF FRENCH COMMUNITY

0   500   1000 miles
0   500   1000   1500 kilometres

Longitude 0 of Greenwich

a. f. de souza 1973

I · A Decade of Coups

A field study tour in 1960-1 – the year of independence as it has been called – to investigate the place of the armed forces in societies in Africa did not, even with hindsight, provide the evidence on which to forecast the eventual spate of coups. The mutiny of the *Force Publique* in the Congo had, however, already taken place and in December 1960 the Imperial Guard in Ethiopia made an attempt to overthrow the Emperor. These were events in fact in two very different categories – a mutiny about pay and particularly promotion and a full-blooded attempt to overthrow the existing civil order. But they indicated a potential and a propensity which on the basis of experience in other parts of the world should perhaps have not been unexpected. It was not, however, until 1963 that, in Togo, Congo (Brazzaville) and Dahomey, the new reality began to take shape. Between January 1963 and the end of February 1966 there were fourteen significant cases of political intervention by the military. By early 1968 there had been nineteen successful military coups and by the end of 1970 the total number of relevant major incidents in Africa in eight years was near to thirty.

No elaborately structured analysis of these events is necessary as a preliminary to asserting that each and every one was, *sui generis*, defying clear-cut categorization except by essentially meretricious devices. Indeed, the difficulty in arriving at a reliable and acceptable figure for the aggregate of military mutinies, coups, transfers of power, take-overs, secessions and plots is itself symptomatic of this fact. This is not to say that some broad classifications of the circumstances in which coups take place and of the motives of the military are not practicable and helpful to our understanding, but each fresh outbreak has so far presented new features and, therefore, a new problem of analysis. To justify this claim it is not necessary to look further than the bizarre Ivory Coast plot of June 1973.

The Ivorian case arose in the African country which more than any other had been persuaded to accept the virtues of a stability based on Western norms of prosperity and external relations. President Houphoüet-Boigny had, ever since his country somewhat belatedly inherited units of the French army, succeeded in keeping the military in the background in spite of the probability that a few of the younger officers impatient for promotion must have looked with envy at the performance of their contemporaries in neighbouring Upper Volta, Mali, Togo and Dahomey. Moreover, the rewards of their civil counterparts in public services and enterprises of various kinds were clearly in a different and superior class to their own admittedly comfortable salaries. Unlike many of their contemporaries in other countries, they worked in the context of a viable economy where progress in development could be measured, and a pacific foreign policy ensured a militarily unexciting rôle. A promotion block deriving from a reluctance to discharge many senior officers of standing and the continuing presence of not insignificant numbers of French advisers were, however, clear sources of dissatisfaction. It could be argued that the timing of these familiar grievances unusually long after independence was a sign that the authorities had paid insufficient attention to the erection of a truly national military institution. As a result of the plot they had to face up to the not unfamiliar dilemma of how to keep the armed forces quietly happy without inflating their prestige and thereby encouraging an improvement in their status to the point where it might affect the character of the régime.

It might with some justice be claimed that the Ivory Coast plot simply reflected the continuing influence of the colonial legacy and that the roots of discontent revealed were in some senses typical. But there was little evidence in this case of a convergence between military grievances and civil unrest. The Ivory Coast had maintained a reputation for peace and stability: this may have been achieved by some sacrifice of positive nationalism and under-enthusiasm, in the eyes of a minority, for pan-African ideals, but there were no indications of the plotters' concern on these scores. What was remarkable was the plotters' eschewing of normal military techniques in their somewhat hazy preparations for the coup and their corresponding failure to capitalize on the basic administrative skills, so widely believed to be the military's main attributes, in planning their violent seizure of power. The extent of their reliance on the supernatural and human sacrifice was unique. No corresponding case of a military cabal abandoning the normal claim to be the agents of modernization and modernity and reverting to the modes of a primitive culture comes to mind. Nor is it likely that a state so careful of its image as the Ivory Coast deliberately exaggerated the superstitious and gruesome character of these surprising events.

Clearly the full range of possible scenarios for military intervention in Africa is not yet complete and unforeseen combinations of circumstances are likely to produce fresh surprises. A frequently underrated factor has been the effective presence at a given time of a single personality whose personal idiosyncrasy, skill or unscrupulous opportunism or possibly his state of mental or physical health has changed the course of events. In the context of a study of military régimes General Idi Amin of Uganda is an obvious case in point, as will be seen later: so too in the opposite sense proved Jomo Kenyatta, whose attitude towards the army seems to have been of paramount importance for the stability of Kenya.

Looking back to the starting point of independence in 1960–1 it was possible even then, when the image of the military was generally negative, to discern an awareness in the minds of particular individuals of the political potential of armies. Kwame Nkrumah's initial reluctance, until external factors brought about a change or overrode his instinctive caution, rapidly to Africanize his officer corps indicated his awareness of the dilemma of which Julius Nyerere was to be made acutely conscious at the time of the East African mutinies in 1964. Nyerere himself frankly admitted to taking his cue from Nkrumah. Moreover, before independence Nyerere debated the need for a conventional military establishment at all. In both cases the possibility of undesirable military activity in the political field was clearly in their minds: this is likely to have had some bearing on Nyerere's search for a new style of people's army in the Chinese mode. Elsewhere – for example, in some quarters in Sierra Leone – a combination of pacific inclinations with a logical realism about the military effectiveness of very small forces induced a brief debate on the necessity of an army but the hesitations were generally short-lived in the face of the excitements of state-founding.

Rare indeed were the cases in which the withdrawing colonial power attempted deliberately to educate its successors in the conventional merits of the military as an organ of state. Of the Commonwealth leaders, only Julius Nyerere took the salute at a military parade before independence: this was a direct consequence of the exceptional character of his relationship with his colonial mentors. And only in Nigeria was the feeling for the army's political potential in any sense acute. The French military schools were popular, but where else except Nigeria had young Africans pressed for the establishment of voluntary military training units in universities and other institutions of higher education? The authorities, not unnaturally, expressed some reservations about the possible presence of quantities of small arms on the campus. Such pressures were in line with the tone of discussion prevailing soon after Nigerian independence about the means of resolving regional political rivalries. The view that a strong man would arise and act with the support of the army was sufficiently widely expressed amongst, for example, Yorubas in the army, for a visitor to be aware of the undercurrent. In retrospect, the interest shown in the establishment of some form of military studies at the new university at Nsukka and Colonel Ojukwu's switch from the civil service to the army in 1957 certainly have some significance. The latter's conviction that the country's interest would be best served by a public service college in which cadets for all services, civil as well as military, would receive basic education and training was a measure of the comprehensiveness of his understanding of the civil–military problem. There were voices – notably Chiefs Awolowo and H. O. Davies, Q.C. – who cautioned the country against the dangers of a substantial military establishment, the former citing the Dominican Republic as a warning. In most ex-colonies, however, ignorance of the military rather than awareness of its potential prevailed and this was one important factor throughout the continent tending politically to neutralize the military for an interval after independence.

It was probably the traditional abhorrence of military rule – strongest in countries like Britain – which caused military intervention generally to be regarded as an aberration with criminal overtones. Whatever its merits and moral justification, however, it is now statistically justifiable to regard military rule as a norm rather than a deviant, certainly in comparison with any other satisfactorily defined form of government. That being so it becomes necessary to explain its relative rarity in newly independent Africa until the beginning of 1966. One factor has already been mentioned and the complete explanation is not hard to find. Roger Murray* succinctly described the weaknesses of the new military establishments as 'expatriate officers, anachronistic equipment, inglorious responsibilities, paucity of authentic tradition'. The armies of Africa needed time to gain acceptance as potentially legitimate

* In 'Militarism in Africa', *New Left Review* 38, July–August 1968, 37.

national leaders. The assumed stereotype of the military officer as essentially dedicated to the public interest, patriotic and perhaps austerely puritanical and capable of self-denial is an apparently far cry from the attitudes prevailing at independence. There had been a legacy of fear and distrust of soldiers in many areas. Nationalist politicians saw them as agents of imperial rule suppressing political demonstrations and protecting European property. Though they had won glory by serving overseas in the two world wars, their imperial activities caused them to be regarded in some quarters as armies of occupation or at best as mercenaries in the service of a foreign power. This impression was assisted by a recruitment policy which preferred subjectively defined 'martial races' or those who were 'worthwhile as soldiers'. The ensuing tribal imbalance necessarily made more difficult than it would otherwise have been the army's achievement of national status as an institution. The presence after independence of a high proportion of expatriate officers even in executive positions not only reinforced these factors, but also provided in practice a major obstacle to conspiracy and unconstitutional action.

Partly because the military had no positive rôle to play in the process of decolonization and the achievement of independence, the rate of Africanization of senior posts in the armed services fell far behind that in the civil administrative sector of government. The localization of the officer corps had a low priority not only in the minds of politicians, who sometimes, as has been seen, were worried about the consequences, but also amongst families and individuals from whom the necessary recruits might have been drawn. Of all the tropical African countries only the Sudan had at the moment of independence a significant proportion of African officers. In that case local military training had been provided by the British since 1918. By contrast, even Ghana with its relatively large educated élite had only about 10 per cent indigenous army officers in March 1957. The case of the *Force Publique* in the Belgian

Congo is well known: the complete lack of any African officers in a force totalling in July 1960 more than 24,000 men and General Janssen's unresponsive attitude to the problem immediately after independence were themselves enough to provoke a mutiny. The Tanzanian and Ugandan mutinies of 1964 had their roots in a similar but less dramatic situation.

In retrospect the initial shortage of African officers was due in detail to the shortage of appropriately educated recruits – a phrase which itself begs an important question – which was in turn in part attributable to anti-military sentiments, and in general to the natural unwillingness of the imperial powers to contemplate local control of defence before self-government had been finally granted. Even that event brought no immediate change because a radical military reorganization could hardly claim the highest priority and, as Patrice Lumumba put it, 'We are not, just because the Congo is independent, going to turn a second-class soldier into a general'.* The new leaders of Africa were generally anxious to have at their disposal organizations which were recognizable, knew their place and rôle, and were not in the throes of violent change. Financial difficulties in any case inhibited military spending, but the demands of national pride as well as external influences changed the pattern.

Once these now obvious braking factors were removed coups took place, and there have been many attempts systematically to account for their occurrence and frequency. Some analysts have concentrated on the organizational characteristics of armies. Others have maintained that these were largely irrelevant, claiming that military behaviour is determined by the social and political condition of the society in which they are operating. This is the view of Professor Samuel P. Huntington, expressed in his book, *Political Order in Changing Societies*,†

* Quoted in Catherine Hoskyns, *The Congo Since Independence*, London, 1965, 60.
† New Haven, Conn., 1969, 192 *et seq.*

in which he also claims that the actual political character of the military intervention is similarly decided:

> As society changes, so does the rôle of the military. In the world of oligarchy, the soldier is a radical; in the middle-class world he is a participant and arbiter; as the mass society looms on the horizon he becomes the conservative guardian of the existing order. . . . The extent to which a politicized officer corps plays a conservative or reform rôle in politics is a function of the expansion of political participation in society.

Apart from the oversimplification of the process of political development implicit in this statement, there is an inherent failure to distinguish between military institutions in different societies and a clear assumption that the officer corps are necessarily middle-class orientated and never identify with the masses, whoever they may be. The diversity of cases suggests that it is safer and more profitable to assume interactions of differing proportions between the military micro-organism and the socio-political system of which it is a part. The general proposition that military take-overs in Africa reflect urban and intellectual discontent, as well as a vacuum of national power and infrastructural underdevelopment within recently independent states, while being at the same time the product of the characteristics of particular military sub-communities and their leaders, seems a reasonable hypothesis with which to begin.

Even to draw a distinction between the military institutions and the social structure of the society within which it operates is to a degree misleading: the armed forces, especially in small and less developed states, are an integral part of that structure and their leadership élite is not in many ways significantly differentiated from their opposite numbers in the civil service, state enterprises, commerce and industry. At the same time the military do possess special qualities and skills and it is their deployment of them or the exploitation of them by others which makes intervention in politics practicable.

The assumption that unnecessarily large armed forces – unnecessary that is for the fulfilment of defence functions strictly defined – lead to the militarization of society may be tenable. Its apparent corollary, that the size of armed forces in relation to the total population of a country has a direct bearing on the likelihood of army intervention in politics, has not been borne out by African experience. As already indicated, financial and other considerations, particularly initially, have restricted expansion. The colonial legacy in this respect was very slight and though inevitably there have been substantial increases in many cases, only Nigeria, in the aftermath of civil war, and possibly one or two other countries, such as Ethiopia, have large armed forces by global standards. As the original Togo affair in January 1963 showed, a minimal force can effectively transfer power from one civilian group to another. What is affected by the number of trained men in uniform is the character of a military administration consequent upon a coup. Generally régimes such as those established in Ghana by Colonel Kotoka initially, and in 1972 by Colonel Acheampong, have relied heavily on the permanent civil service as much out of necessity as of choice. This seems to be the common African pattern, and in this respect even Nigeria has so far proved no exception.

Whatever their motivation or the local circumstances coups in Africa have been strikingly similar in terms of their mechanics. As in other parts of the world the radio and cable stations, major telephone exchanges and key government buildings have been the revolutionaries' immediate objectives. They have, however, often relied unusually heavily on the co-operation of the police even to provide communication facilities, and even where aircraft and tanks have been available they do not generally seem to have been central to the plan. For the initial strike military or requisitioned civil aircraft seem to have played practically no part. The technical expertise deployed has not extended beyond the basic maintenance of road transport, radio communication, bridge building and occasionally demolition. In other words the assumed goodwill and co-operation of technicians and engineers concerned with the power industry and water supply has been fundamental to success. At the same time, with certain notable exceptions, African coups over the last decade have been relatively blood-less. This must reflect largely on their popular acceptability at the time, but it is also probably in some measure attributable to the administrative training which plays such a large part in the officer development programmes of the imperial mentors – primarily Britain and France.

To describe African armed forces as the channels of technical modernization and innovation in the sense which armies else-where have sometimes proved to be is to ignore the facts. Hardly a single country in Sub-Saharan Africa has any capacity for this kind of training except through universities, and the total number of graduate officers is small indeed; the number of African officers who have successfully undertaken the standard science and engineering training provided for special-ist British officers is minute and at French hands not sub-stantial. On the other hand, the application of well-mastered administrative procedures to the initial execution and to the day-to-day administration in the post-coup phase has on the whole been impressive. Not only has control in highly volatile situations apparently avoided much bloodshed and, therefore, recriminations and festering bitterness, but in a number of places, notably the Nigerian states, military men have proved adept in sustaining the commercial life of the area.

What was a tentative assumption is now, at least on the grounds of amassed indirect evidence, virtually proven – namely, that simple administrative procedures well learned and almost unthinkingly applied work well up to a point in the context of the relatively unsophisticated state structures of the less developed countries. Their utility in the establishment of a military régime is now scarcely in question; but their demerits over the longer term, when policy needs to be evolved and the undercurrents of popular opinion require to be tested and appeased, are features of some of the cases, studies of which follow. The truths that national economic problems do not consist of clear-cut choices between obvious alternatives and that to neglect consultation, however tedious and time consuming, may make an otherwise valid decision inoperative, are not easily appreciated by those used to the issue of straightforward instructions by superior to subordinate within a strict hierarchy. The Ghana case illustrates well the pitfalls this can create in dealings with a civil service whose behaviour in any case may have been adversely conditioned in the matter of the exercise of discretion by the pre-coup climate. The peculiar skills of the military have been regularly shown to induce a sense of separateness which may isolate them at a time when the need for identification is paramount in order to overcome the barriers set up by the physical segregation of armies created in an élitist tradition.

The inherent weaknesses and strengths of the military in politics are thus well exposed. The very segregation which is on the achievement of power a potential liability is an important factor in making a coup practicable. The army camp – on the outskirts of a town but separate from it or in a so-called cantonment – is secure against intrusion and its occupants do not generally have to justify their actions or their movements. This circumstance facilitated the nearly successful counter-coup in Ghana in April 1967; it certainly made practicable the various and diverse Nigerian army interventions in different parts of the country in January and July 1966 as well as conspicuously aiding the conspirators in March 1967 in Sierra Leone, where the army has its barracks poised symbolically on the ridge overlooking the capital, Freetown. The pretext of training exercises and manoeuvres enhances the facility of exclusive isolation. In Ghana in February 1966 and April 1967 this was the overt excuse for troop movements, while Major Nzeogwu's attack on the house of the Sardauna at Kaduna in Northern Nigeria in fact seems to have been well rehearsed as well as eventually implemented in this guise. This and the convenience of the officers' mess have in British- and French-influenced Africa facilitated coups. The mess indeed symbolizes the profession because it is exclusive and its members by definition have control over entry to it and of the rules and conventions which operate within it. Hence the traumatic impact on the Ghana army of Kwame Nkrumah's attempt to insinuate political agents into this professional shrine, particularly in the guise of NCOs and other ranks. It would, however, be a mistake to assume that plotting took place on any broad basis.

It is still true to say that the remarkable feature of most African coups has been the very small number of people with a knowledge of the plans before the day and the corresponding sureness of the response of their colleagues and of the popular reception. Though there is, for example, some doubt now about the initiative for the initial Ghana coup in February 1966 – did it come from Harlley or Kotoka? – the small size of the group concerned remains undisputed and similarly with the Nigerian and other episodes.

All this, however, is essentially a matter of procedure and opportunity, it is not the substance of the question. Viewed objectively there have now been many chances to observe the emergence of armed forces in Africa as a political force. A decade and more ago they were not thought to have a routine place in the political system of an emergent state in that continent. Today they have secured a quasi-constitutional position – often as a result of appearing to be the only alternative government in a one-party system, particularly where the head of state has acquired or appears to be on the verge of acquiring life tenure. As coup has followed coup, especially within a single state, the pretence of acting in defence of the original constitution – a reality to some of the early coup leaders – has gradually slipped away. The larger claim of acting in the interests of the people to remove an unsatisfactory ruler has tended to replace it. The nature of the régime's deficiencies is rarely at the time of take-over clearly defined: their cataloguing and enumeration are matters for subsequent enquiries which help to keep the virtues of the usurpers in the public mind. It has, however, become possible to discern a range of factors which in various combinations indicate favourable omens for a coup, provided that at the same time the military themselves are not lacking the stimuli to intervene. It could well be argued that in less developed countries 'with a low level of political culture' armies take over the reins in emergency conditions where in Western democracies there would be a call for some kind of national coalition: it might even cynically be suggested that practice has made the coup seem a simpler process than the forging of fragile political alliances. The charge that repetition and ease of execution may turn it into an irresponsible habit whenever there are problems even of moderate difficulty or factional or personal plans and ambitions are thwarted is not impossible to sustain: as early as December 1969 the army had intervened five times in Dahomey and the episodic series continues with monotonous regularity, from the observer's point of view.

Economic stagnation and a depressed standard of living do not of themselves generate military coups. If this were true then their frequency would be even greater than it is. Even though many African states are of doubtful economic viability and in most, partly because of the continuing prevalence of expatriate élite standards of income and living, there is an exceptionally wide gap between rich and poor, this is no infallible indicator of impending military intervention. It does, however, help to account for the relatively greater frequency of coups in less-developed as opposed to more-developed countries.

Failure to achieve the expected rapid development after the nationalist triumph of independence is one cause for the dispersion of euphoria. Since 1960 fluctuations in the world price of primary products, unemployment amongst school leavers and financial extravagance and mismanagement have been fairly widespread in Africa. Discontent at high prices and at shortages due to the imposition of import controls has provided the tinder which the spark of an austerity budget has ignited in a number of countries, including Ghana. In the Togo Republic in 1963 when President Olympio was murdered, and a few months later in Congo (Brazzaville) when President Fulbert Youlou was overthrown, unemployment played its part. In Dahomey, in October 1963, a general strike and widespread labour troubles focussed discontent and, subsequently, the almost inevitable failure to satisfy the demands of a sufficient number of the influential sectors of the community, including the armed forces, led to a repeat performance. On the other hand, in Upper Volta in 1966, Colonel Lamizana intervened to safeguard democratic institutions in the face of labour disorder. It has even been suggested that one factor affecting army intervention in Nigeria in 1966 was that the unions were in such a state of disarray that they were failing to exercise appropriate political influence on the government. In Ghana a succession of austerity budgets resulting largely from overspending on prestige projects eventually helped to create the climate for a successful coup even though at the time the unions had not themselves reacted strongly.

Economic discontents have undoubtedly provided a backcloth conducive to the performance of military coups but because, for the most part, military governments have only been able to apply palliatives and certainly not proved competent to achieve economic viability in the short term, they have soon become just as much a threat to the new régime as to the old one. The evidence suggests that the impact of austerity measures on the perquisites of the privileged has had a more profound influence than the struggles of the poor. This indicates the probably greater significance of broadly based political disillusionment as compared with specific economic grievance.

The educated middle class in Africa as elsewhere were in any case the most likely to react against attempts by a dominant party to maintain unanimity once the colonial power had withdrawn. When resort was made to force or preventive detention was introduced to mute anti-government criticism and to destroy the opposition, they were the critics of oppression and of the denial of effective political choice. Inevitably, political parties geared to the achievement of independence failed to adapt adequately to the needs of a self-governing African state. At the same time the appurtenances of democracy and the luxury of impartial civil servants seemed to some leaders time-wasting obstacles to the basic tasks of development and nation building. Where, as in most African countries, and particularly Nigeria, local ethnic allegiances were involved and loomed larger with an increased interest in political participation, opposition was likely to take obsessive, even violent, forms. The results were unwise and unrealistic attempts to restore unity by force and the use of force itself enhanced the importance of those officially charged with its deployment, the police and the military. In turn the status and authority of the political parties and the civil service were undermined. Moreover, the official deployment of force in whatever form is almost inevitably of diminishing utility. In these circumstances power concentrated in the hands of a single person or an oligarchy creates schisms within the government party and the country. The military's status as a national institution inclines it to stand for unity and against schism whether it derives from personal or regional rivalries. It was, therefore, understandable that in Ghana, for example, the suppressed opposition party which had been a rallying point for a diversity of the aggrieved should after Nkrumah's overthrow revive and become the agency through which the military sought the return to civilian rule. Elsewhere, Generals Soglo in Dahomey and Mobutu in Zaïre sought 'to restore a political equilibrium which had been disrupted by personal conflicts'.* Their expectations of forming 'caretaker' governments which would simply hold the ring and restore the *status quo* were not fulfilled but in some measure realistically reflected the limited political potential of a military government.

The growing frequency of military interventions in politics after 1963 raised the question of infection or contagion from one country to another across Africa. The testimony one way or another is slight and we can only speculate and consider what is merely circumstantial evidence. Normal intercourse across state frontiers was in any case increasing, especially between those speaking the same European language. More significantly, African army officers had legitimate opportunities to meet and correspond, which arose from their shared educational and training experiences overseas. On the face of it, however, the direct links between one coup and another were small. Helen Kitchen† cites an interesting case relating to Colonel David Thompson, commanding officer of Liberia's National Guard who was arrested on suspicion of plotting a coup and is alleged to have said three weeks after President Olympio had been assassinated in Togo, 'If only 250 Togolese soldiers could overthrow their government a Liberian army of 5000 could seize power easily'. An examination of the chronology of African coups does give some slight support for the notion of a degree of regional contagion if one assumes that this is the significance of 'clusters' of coups in given years.

It does, however, seem more likely that the removal of the fear of external intervention, notably by the former colonial

* Claude E. Welch, 'Soldier and state in Africa' in *Journal of Modern African Studies*, Vol. 5, No. 3, 1967, 316.
† In 'Filling the Togo Vacuum', *Africa Report*, VIII, 2, January 1963, 9.

power, was an important factor between 1963 and 1966. The withdrawal of expatriate personnel from executive positions was the first stage. Early in 1964 came the East African mutinies in Tanganyika, Uganda and Kenya: British troops intervened effectively at local request and Julius Nyerere in particular was courageous enough publicly to express his thanks for their invited action. Later that year in somewhat different circumstances the French government authorized intervention to suppress a rising against President Mba's régime in Gabon. Since that time, in spite of French assistance to Tombalbaye's government in Chad, there has been a marked reluctance on the part of the former colonial powers to involve themselves in such enterprises. The British government has retained little local capacity for speedy intervention and French forces have been progressively withdrawn from the continent though a highly mobile formation has been retained in France for such purposes. The philosophy that military assistance should be provided apparently to maintain stability in an area at the request of a legitimate and well-established government seemed to involve the corollary that popularly (however defined) supported coups should be allowed to run their course. But the rapidity with which successful coups are executed and the fact that Africa is not of prime concern for the security of the relevant European powers – unless there is an incident with major international implications – has in practice meant that France, and certainly Britain, have remained spectators on the sidelines from which they are increasingly unlikely to move even on grounds of political expediency. The suspicion that in certain cases they have actually promoted a coup in order to eliminate a régime unsympathetic to their interests has yet to be substantiated.

The charge of corruption and misappropriation is frequently made to justify military coups in Africa as elsewhere. The question is not whether it exists – it is clearly endemic in the majority of states – but whether it is of any great importance in inducing military intervention. This is essentially a matter of political behaviour. In a poor community conspicuous expenditure may be an incitement to protest and violence on the part of those who are deprived, though there may also be subconscious admiration of those who are able as it were 'to get away with it'. It may well be asked whether relatively comfortably placed army personnel living in what were European-style residential areas are necessarily affected by this. A blatant manifestation of extravagance at the time of an austerity budget is obviously impolitic and President Yameogo in Upper Volta appears to have disregarded popular sensitivities in this way. It seems now to be generally accepted that Chief Festus Okotie Eboh, Federal Finance Minister in Nigeria, would not have been selected for abduction and murder if his financial manoeuvres had not appeared unusually reprehensible. Both sets of military coup leaders in Ghana have made allegations against their civilian predecessors, Drs Nkrumah and Busia respectively, that they and particularly their supporters misused public money for personal advantage. Commissions of inquiry in that country have revealed apparent scandals, but it is important not to confuse cause with retrospective justification. The only certainty in this respect is that military régimes who stress the corruption of those they have overthrown are the more likely to have the charge turned against them if they fail to live up to their own precepts.

The general conclusion then must be that economic problems, corruption, political schism and general disillusionment have combined to create the climate in which coups can successfully take place. It is, however, apparent that in Africa such events have in general terms been as much related to the distribution of power in society. There is also evidence from a number of countries that there is concern for the standing of the state in the eyes of the world and that when things go awry it is natural to accept intervention by the army because it is seen as patriotic by definition and possessed of unusual virtue and rectitude. The important thing, however, is that the crisis when the army ceases to be the willing instrument of the government of a recently independent state and takes over its powers seems to come when the military feel threatened as an institution or when they are required to carry out policies which are unacceptable on behalf of politicians whose personal or public conduct is distasteful. The case history of the Ghana army contains all the necessary ingredients, commencing with involvement in political machinations in the Congo which seemed in the circumstances unprofessional and abhorrent. Arbitrary decisions to train officers in a new mode, e.g. in Russia as opposed to Britain, to retire senior officers and replace them with the personal choice of the head of state, reduction of privileges and amenities, creation of a rival security force, a threat to involve the defence forces in a risky foreign adventure, and above all interference with the professional autonomy of the army – some of these factors are to be found in many cases.

Sometimes, however, the causes of unrest have sprung from within the defence forces themselves. In Africa as many coups or attempted coups have been the products of fissions within the military as of the cohesion of that body. Inter-generational or inter-tribal tensions have played their part in Mali, Dahomey, Ghana, Nigeria, the Congo Republic, Burundi and elsewhere. Factional military interests in the context of socio-economic discontent have proved as effective as the solidarity of the armed forces and must be taken into account in any attempt to construct a general model of the factors and elements, both proximate and long-term, which are likely to trigger a military seizure of power.

The history of civil–military relations in the embryonic states of Africa since 1960 has exposed more clearly than ever before the range of variables involved in determining military decisions to intervene in the politics of their countries and their possible effectiveness once a decision has been taken. Of primary importance is the composition and nature of the mili-

tary oligarchy. This will have been affected on the one hand by
the circumstances in which the country concerned achieved
independence: clearly the Algerian struggle – a fight for freedom – has left a legacy unlike that in the Ivory Coast, Ghana
or Nigeria where there was a peaceful transfer of power. On
the other hand, political activity or passivity in military circles
may relate to the length and nature of overseas experience in
the service of the colonial power on the part of senior African
officers at the time of independence. Dahomeyan officers who
fought in Indo-China contrast with Malian subalterns too
young to have done so. Within the same officer corps inter-
generational differences have in some cases been compounded
by training under the auspices of different foreign powers and
led to strains on service unity and discipline as well as to
competition for recognition and promotion and possible ideological conflict. Circumstances have so far precluded a satis-
factory evaluation of the different impact on the individual of
officer training received at home or abroad. The consequences
of the establishment of an indigenous military academy after
heavy reliance on, for example, Sandhurst or St Cyr, are as yet
unknown. In what sense, except for routine political instruc-
tion, Communist military training really differs in its impact
from that of Western Europe or the United States is hard to
assess but the possible divergence clearly cannot be ignored.

Important factors which have so far been largely neglected
are interrelated – namely the degree of military preparation
for independence, the state of Africanization of the officer
corps at that date, and the rate of post-independence expansion
of the armed forces. Such criteria are useful in comparing the
behaviour of the military in, for example, Kenya and Uganda
which started from an apparently identical base – the regi-
ments of the imperial King's African Rifles. Related to the
speed of expansion of the armed forces is the attitude of the
civil power – political and official – to budgetary allocations for
new forces, weapons and training programmes which in turn

may have been affected by the nature of the relationships between the armed forces and the bureaucracy at central and
local level. There is evidence too, again from Kenya and
Uganda, that the extent of the continuing links with the
former imperial power may be important, particularly if it is
related to the performance of the new army in dealing with
frontier or internal security problems and the way in which
the political leadership has chosen to deploy it. A partial
answer to the question why intervention has not taken place
in a particular country may lie in these factors.

The fallacy of treating military factors in isolation has already been discussed. Military budgets, for example, are
meaningful only in the context of the established priorities, if
any, for economic and social reform and national development
plans. The political approach to problems of public order is
also relevant, especially the extent of reliance on the military
or police apparatus for intelligence connected with internal
security. The reputation of a régime, even in a small developing
country, depends as much on its apparent external image and
its status, for instance, in the Organization of African Unity as
it does on sophisticated assessments of its domestic effectiveness. Its success or failure in avoiding military intervention
will depend to some extent on its own cohesion, its ability to
reward success, and its attitude to the judiciary and the bureaucracy. It may be prone to make critical errors in assigning the
military to military or non-military rôles within the country –
President Obote of Uganda comes to mind at this point – and
may pay too little attention to the popular view of the defence
services and to the grounds for disaffection within them.

The taxonomy of military coups can thus be made to appear
immensely complex and at the same time largely irrelevant.
The question of their desirability, or otherwise, is in the circumstances a sterile question. What is of interest both to the
countries of Africa and to the student of politics is the extent
to which coups can in any sense further the development, in

the societies in which they occur, of a just, tolerant and consequently perhaps stable socio-political system. The phenomenon of the violent seizure of power is now of less significance there than what is done with it once it has been seized.

II · The Professional Legacy of Colonial Rule

With the benefit of hindsight many observers have come to see the spate of military coups in the 1960s as an inevitable if not particularly desirable part of the process of political development and, in particular, of the evolution of effective centralized national governments in Africa. One of the essential problems of the study of political change and of state and nation building in Africa is to assess the contribution of European colonial rule without judging the new states almost wholly by Western norms. Even the basic terminology, such as the word 'state', is in a sense an alien importation but its adoption is inevitable and not altogether inappropriate provided its limitations in a different cultural context are fully appreciated. An obvious example is that in a state with a strongly differentiated tribal substructure the effectiveness of the authority of the central government and the nature of the subject's loyalty to it will be of a different order from that which is normal in non-tribal Western societies, though even these are sometimes afflicted by the demands of minority and even potentially secessionist ethnic groups. The task of analysis is in some ways made easier and in others more difficult by the fact that most African states are in the hands of élite groups which have publicly declared their acceptance of such alien objectives as economic development and the establishment of authority on a national basis.

This adherence to the vague concept of 'the modern state' and its values may often appear in practice hypocritical but it is nevertheless an important factor in the assessment of political

achievement. Indeed the suggestion sometimes made at the end
of the colonial period that specially modified versions of
Western institutions should be developed in African countries
was generally disdainfully rejected on the grounds that only 'the
best' would do for Africa. The implication was that the best was
that which appeared to give the imperial powers their enormous
material and other advantages over the emerging countries.
Some nationalist leaders, like Kwame Nkrumah, identified
'the political kingdom' as the key to all else, and for this reason
Nkrumah would probably not in the first instance have considered settling for anything other than a Westminster style
parliamentary system entirely manned by African personnel.

Because of the peculiar nature of military institutions, these
considerations applied in a magnified form to the defence and
security services of most African countries. One reason for this
was that until the moment of independence these services were
inevitably the agents of the imperial power for the limitation of
militant political activity and the prevention of insurgency,
and then by an act of transformation became the servants of
political groups whom the day before they had been responsible
for restraining. This was the main reason why the new nationalist leaders often paid little attention to the military arm before
independence and accounted for the relatively slow conversion
of colonial defence forces into national armies. The essentially
mercenary nature of service in these forces in the colonial
period at a time when monetary reward for labour was an ex-
citing and apparently liberating innovation also effectively
created a confusion of loyalties which was reinforced by the
tendency to recruit soldiers from areas remote from the political
turbulence of the towns. The undoubted fact that the African
armies of the 1970s, in spite of expansion, are still with few
exceptions recognizably the same institutions they were in
1960 and are manned, at any rate in the senior ranks, by officers
trained in an imperial environment, makes an examination in
depth of the imperial legacy eminently worthwhile. At the

same time, however, explanations of military political behaviour which attribute almost the whole responsibility to the colonial power must be viewed with great caution, for armies themselves do not often actually create the social circumstances conducive to their intervention in politics.

The recent academic tendency has been to concentrate on the construction of models of political change based on the assumed attributes of the military or on classifications of armies which appear theoretically valid but have little practical relevance. This may be as misleading in this field as the uncritical assumption of cause and effect. Any attempt, therefore, to study the Western contribution to the development of African military systems should involve a definition of basic terms. In the first place, what do we understand by an army? What distinguishes an army from any other body of armed men? This distinction is clearly of particular importance in relation to *coups d'état* for which purpose the possession of arms is the obvious *sine qua non* but in the organization of which other characteristics are apparently of greater moment. It is also possible for an army to decline or deteriorate from that status into a number of bodies of armed men, as the *Force Publique* in the Congo showed.

It is easier to say what an army is not than what it is – thus a modern army 'is not a temporary band of marauders, nor a disorganized militia. Its *raison d'etre* is the rational utilization of violence; its organization reflects the application of modern techniques'.* The validity of the latter part of this statement depends directly on other positive characteristics essential to an army. A first prerequisite would seem to be central control and a chain of command responsible for executive operational and disciplinary measures. A strict hierarchy may, if we examine the few extant examples of true people's armies, not actually be necessary but it is widely accepted as a requirement

* Claude E. Welch in *Soldier and State in Africa*, Northwestern University Press, Evanston, 1970, 39.

and the whole structure would be inoperative if it were not capable of management through some kind of private or independent communications system. Effective action also depends on over-riding loyalties which are associated with a basic concern for some large purpose, generally 'the national interest', though clearly it could be international, ideological or religious. Not only is there this sense of purpose but implicitly a system of internal loyalties, tending in most cases to weaken other allegiances, of a tribal, regional, ethnic or socio-economic nature, which is often known in Western countries as *esprit de corps*. Such an institution, it may be said, is by definition professional and demands control over its own membership and conditions of service: but the terms 'professional' and 'professionalism' themselves require some explanation.

It is indeed questionable whether armies would be generally recognized as particularly vivid symbols of statehood if it were not that their officer corps have acquired the mystique of professionalism. This was not always the case and the historical transition from mercenary, or feudal forces, has been recent even in the West. A profession can be defined as a field of activity which involves something more than long-term commitment and a reasonable level of reward: its members have an obligation to serve society in accordance with a code of duty overriding personal ambition and convenience. It is sometimes referred to as a vocation in the true sense – a rôle to which individuals are called. A professional man is an expert with all that that implies in terms of intellectual activity: he must be fully cognizant of the historical and social contexts of his own occupation and be able to apply his skills in a considerate fashion – considerate, that is, of the needs of society as a whole. This is what in its most highly developed form should make the military officer identify himself with a state of which he can be proud, and involves special training in skills, techniques and social responsibility. The application of his skills is inseparable from the implicit social obligation. Current attempts by research scientists in Britain and the United States to devise an equivalent to the medical Hippocratic Oath are relevant to this discussion. The problem may lie, as perhaps it did particularly acutely in the case of officers like Afrifa involved in the original Ghana coup, in judging the nature of that obligation because *prima facie* a *coup d'état* is an offence against the order of society – a criminal act. Such incidents highlight an essential feature of professional systems – namely the establishment of a set of conventions inculcated through the profession's educational and training institutions.

All professional groups regard themselves as exclusive and in some senses apart from the mass of society. They have a corporate identity born of their training procedures and of their particular duty to society. It is therefore necessary for them to have control over their own membership, over the qualifications for entry to the profession and its codes of conduct. The profession of military officer, unlike most other professions, involves a wide range of different qualifications and expertise, though these are essentially ancillary to the central purpose which is 'the management of violence' in the interests of the state. This is a function which for effective application must draw on a number of academic disciplines in both the natural and social sciences and is unique in being directly related to the state rather than to the needs of individuals within it, though there will always be human consequences. This has led of necessity to a special concern for the corporate identity of the officer corps to enable its members to carry out their duty without fear or favour, which apart from practical convenience in many societies has resulted in the establishment of military communities living physically apart from the rest of society even though marrying into it.

The professional characteristics described above are to some extent ideal and in practice rarely fully achieved. They do nevertheless provide the guidelines and reference points for an assessment of the extent and true nature of the colonial military legacy to developing countries in Africa. Such a discussion will, of course, be complicated by a number of factors. In the first place the military of the various colonial powers may well have had unique characteristics of their own and tended to reproduce their own particular professional ethos. Secondly, the assimilation of professional values across a wide cultural gap was bound to result in distortions due both to general incompatibility and lack of real communication and understanding by both parties. Finally, the fact that military policies in colonial territories before independence were orientated to imperial strategic needs rather than to national development had disruptive consequences not by any means conducive to the development of a new tradition.

As far as Britain is concerned attention has popularly focussed on the rôle of the central officer-training institution – the Royal Military Academy, Sandhurst, the history of which began at about the same time as that of its American equivalent, West Point. It has been said in recent times with some justice that Sandhurst and the former shorter-term officer schools in Britain – Mons Officer Cadet School at Aldershot and Eaton Hall near Chester – have produced more heads of state in Africa and Asia than the London School of Economics, which used to be thought pre-eminent in this respect. This fact has led to misleading and embarrassing assumptions about the nature of the education and training provided at Sandhurst. Critics of Britain as an allegedly neo-colonialist power, for instance, have assumed conscious and deliberate political indoctrination of a conservative or even reactionary ideology – an interpretation which is at least open to doubt.

A direct relationship between this particular type of military training and the achievement of political power is not easy to prove. For one thing, the behavioural characteristics concerned may be common to officers educated in élitist military traditions wherever they are found: there have been enough military coups in the world since the First World War to suggest that this particular form of despotism may be natural and normal rather than some kind of deviation or aberration. In fact, of the fifty-one states recognized in 1917, thirty-two had already experienced military interventions in politics by 1965. Information such as this suggests the difficulty of attempting strictly to distinguish between the effects of the military tradition in general and any particular national form of it. Even if there could be any certainty about the basic proposition, this would throw little light on the real nature of the process: the curriculum and educational environment would still require detailed analysis in order to discover the individual ingredients responsible. An empirical approach to aspects of the British and French experiences in Africa may, however, help to throw light on the question, provided the general characteristics of armies and of military professionalism are borne in mind.

As has already been suggested the specific rôle of Sandhurst may have been exaggerated. Even *The Times* of London headlined an account of General Aguiyi-Ironsi's rise to power 'Test of the Sandhurst Manner', before going on to describe how he had been trained at Eaton Hall. In fact, however, Ironsi was in many ways a typical African product of the British system of military training in that he attended all the relevant courses for regular officer development beyond the cadet stage, including the then Imperial Defence College. It might not be unreasonable to attribute his assumption of office in dangerous circumstances to a sense of inescapable duty to the state cultivated by his professional experience. Other African heads of state trained in Britain have been General Yakubu Gowon, Ironsi's successor in Nigeria, Lieutenant-General A. A. Afrifa, Chairman of the National Liberation Council in Ghana before the return to civilian rule in 1969, and Colonel Juxon-Smith, who presided over the National Reformation Council in Sierra Leone in 1967–8. Several of the senior military administrators in Nigeria from 1966 to 1969, including Hassan Katsina and David Ejoor who were military governors of the Northern and Mid-West regions respectively, were also trained at Sandhurst, and almost all the others were under British auspices in different ways or at other levels: Colonel Ojukwu, the Biafran leader, first graduated at Oxford University before going through some of the later stages of the normal training routine.

All this looks like strong evidence of a connection between training and political behaviour but it is well to remember that the conduct of British trained officers the world over has not been apparently consistent. It is sufficient to quote the cases in Asia of India and Malaysia where the armed forces have generally remained politically passive, and Pakistan where for twelve years they dominated the political scene and are still a potentially obtrusive force. It may even be possible eventually in former British Africa to distinguish between politically reluctant and politically avid officer corps. If so, the conditions in which training and professional values have interacted with local political and social circumstances are likely to prove significant. The state structures, like the military institutions, of the new Commonwealth African states have derived directly from the administrative fabric set up during the colonial period. The transfer of a professional code has in the process been complicated by another pattern of allegiance – deriving from ethnic heterogeneity in many areas – and by the exceptional importance of political power in parts of the world where it is the only reliable route to the acquisition of wealth. The process of transfer of professionalism in this sense has, moreover, been retarded by the shortage of indigenous officers at the time of independence. The emergence of a national army can scarcely begin until the departure of expatriate officers, while their presence was one support for the development of a professional tradition, especially to the extent that it tended to inhibit the explicit politicization of the force.

The slow Africanization of officer corps before independence not surprisingly has proved an inhibition to the development of a stable military establishment, as sophisticated comparisons between Sierra Leone, Ghana, Nigeria, Kenya, Uganda and Tanzania may well eventually show to great effect. It does not seem to have been a result of deliberate imperial policy nor to have been wholly attributable to the slow spread of education and the consequent caution of expatriate officers engaged in recruitment and selection who could not find enough young men in their own image. Had the African political leaderships generally paid more attention to the military arm before independence and thus made it more respectable as a career, it would not have remained for so long a symbol of the imperial régime unable to attract its fair share of the ablest of young men.

The fact that only in Tanganyika, Sierra Leone and, in due course, more effectively in the Gambia was the need for conventional armed forces. ever fundamentally questioned indicates a general acceptance of an alien conception of the needs of a modern state. Alternative means for the maintenance of internal security were in some cases at hand – in the form in the cases of Kenya and Zambia, in particular, of specially trained and equipped units of the police – but with the exception of Gambia, Botswana, Lesotho and Swaziland regular military forces were invariably established. This somewhat inchoate appreciation of armed forces as a symbol of statehood, whether in a ceremonial or operational rôle, became more explicit after independence and it is not surprising that African populations have been willing to regard their armies, at any rate temporarily, as especially patriotic and as the repositories of moral rectitude and a disinterested sense of duty. Implicit in the decisions to establish regular armies in a number of territories was an acceptance of a distinctive rôle for the army, as opposed to the police: not only was this a facet of the British tradition which had a direct and beneficial bearing on the government's relationships with the population in a coercive rôle but it helped to cultivate the notion of the army as a kind of *deus ex machina* capable of resolving complex and deteriorating situations.

The idea of the army as a symbol of the national interest essential to the realization of independence was reinforced in several cases by the coincidence of modern Africa's first international military crisis with the achievement of freedom from colonial rule: the United Nations intervention in the Congo in 1960 was seen as requiring substantial participation by the armed forces of African states. Not only would incapacity to contribute to the UN force have been a blow to national pride, but the operation in the Congo provided a still largely unique opportunity to obtain experience and prove professional competence. Thus while the resolution of the military agnostics, Sierra Leone and Tanganyika, was hardened by this eventuality, the army and police contingents of Ghana and Nigeria had an unusual opportunity to prove their worth. The international press commented favourably on the standard of discipline in the forces of the two countries, which was partly due to the example which they set in the application of skills learned in British training schools. The Congo operation was essentially an exercise in civil–military relations which involved the use of the internal security techniques which are a prominent feature of British military training: these the Ghanaians were able proudly to demonstrate to the Swedish and Irish contingents. Response to the authority of the UN Command involved the exercise of professional judgment when Nkrumah attempted to direct the activities of his own force, and the feeling on the part of able African officers that this interference had reached levels which affected their professional reputation was undoubtedly one factor in generating long-term anti-political discontent in the Ghana army. This was no doubt strengthened by the army's growing confidence in the quality of its own training, generated by the opportunities to display its skill in intra-Commonwealth operations.

The fact that the armies handed over by Britain to African

states were barely adequate to meet the internal needs of newly independent states and certainly insufficient to support aggressive foreign policies may in itself have been a kind of anti-militarist professional recommendation. Historically the small armies were due to the subordination of regional problems to an imperial strategic plan by which metropolitan or other colonial troops could be moved in the event of an emergency. Co-operation between Commonwealth contingents in the Congo was made practicable by the resulting standardization of organization, equipment and command procedure deriving from a common source. This tended to strengthen the attachment of African officers to their military *alma mater*.

An organic military tradition was passed on, as far as it could be, by the agents of British imperial power because it was what they were familiar with and presumably admired. They genuinely saw its values as likely to assist the maintenance of law and order and the development of stable institutions in new states. In other and more practical ways, however, they were not concerned with and certainly largely unaware of the long-term interests of the potential successor states. Conditioned to an illusion of the permanence of imperial rule which lasted at least until 1947, British officials gave absolute priority to the fulfilment of imperial commitments and therefore judged the appropriateness of policies by the criteria of strategic need and local security arrangements. Subconscious political attitudes and personal biases combined to cause the adoption of, for example, recruiting policies which have operated in the longer term against the stability of the ex-colonies. The volunteer mercenary soldier, preferably Moslem and illiterate and almost certainly from the less accessible parts of a territory, was preferred. Such a man was likely to be politically unsophisticated and capable of impartial action against 'alien' urban dwellers. In addition, experience in India had appeared to lend convenient support to a theory that peoples and tribes fell neatly into martial and non-martial classes. This was in line with the seemingly traditional anti-intellectualism prevalent in British military circles until very recently, and amounted to a touching faith in the political innocence of those who were relatively untouched by Western civilization. Thus the Baganda, Kikuyu and the Ibo, who were avid for education whoever provided it, were distrusted as potential soldiers in the same way as Bengalis and Madrassis had been in India.

The resulting situation was fraught with irony, paradox and, more sadly, tragic consequences. In Northern Nigeria the resistance of the Islamic Fulani emirs to the introduction of Western education, when advocated by Lord Lugard in the early 1920s, came to be regarded by British administrators almost as a virtue. The artificial encouragement of local languages, namely Hausa and Swahili, demonstrably inhibited technological progress. The protection of traditional interests on a regional basis was certainly assisted by adherence to other rank-recruiting policies based on quotas from provinces, tribes or districts and even to some extent in West Africa by the enlistment of men from French-speaking territories. When, however, the prospect of independence stimulated the search for African officers, the expatriate selection boards inevitably turned to men educated at least to secondary level in British type schools often largely staffed by Britons. In Nigeria, Uganda and Kenya the consequent differences in the ethnic composition of the other ranks and the officer corps magnified political tensions which in the first two countries have had disastrous or near-disastrous results, and which only the statesmanship and anticipation of President Kenyatta has avoided in Kenya.

The procurement of African officers was at best slow before independence because of the application of European criteria to the process of selection; it was possibly also due to a lack of a sense of urgency on anyone's part and certainly to the rival attractions of other careers. The relative slowness as well as the nature of the process itself led to the creation of a military establishment highly receptive to the élite tradition of which it was clearly the heir. The British, and also the French, moulded officers for the new African defence services who were to an extent replicas of themselves, superficially at least. This does not mean that they developed extra-African loyalties, but rather that they absorbed aspects of an alien professional code and subsequently made military and political judgments which were at least so influenced, as their own political and social institutions had a very short time in which to take root – in many cases, no more than about sixty years in all. As a result, such a peculiar feature as the British style officers' mess was precariously established, though it has in fact in places survived twelve or more years of independence.

The strength of the attachment of individuals in African élites to some of the modes and conventions of Western societies derived from the spread of education in schools which were imitations – sometimes very good imitations – of their European counterparts. Such schools seemed to fit much more naturally into the cultural pattern of Africa than they had in India and South Asia generally: their emphasis was automatically on liberal academic rather than technical or vocational education, now a matter for regret in, for example, Colonel Acheampong's Ghana. In this respect, the British and the French differed from the Belgians who concentrated on the economic possibilities in educating Africans in the Congo and thus created a different kind of vacuum to be filled after independence. The affinity between educated Africans generally and Britain and France is, therefore, marked. To some extent, of course, one's view is coloured by one's political standpoint: Marxist writers have described Ghanaian officers as 'Anglo-African', using arguments analogous to those employed by Frantz Fanon in *The Wretched of the Earth*, and by Jean-Paul Sartre in the introduction to that book. The pertinent question is clearly whether these men have proved 'loyal Africans' or have to some extent distorted the political development of their own societies because of their absorption of alien values.

Assessment of the effects of foreign training can only be empirical and to some extent speculative. There is not a great deal of first-hand evidence of the reactions to such training except the generalized and stereotyped responses obtainable from time to time in radio or television interviews. Deduction from the behaviour of individuals or the conduct of governments is necessarily the main source of understanding which may be much facilitated by comparative studies. A very few active participants in military coups have expressed their own feelings: two of the Ghana coup leaders, Colonel A. A. Afrifa and Major-General A. K. Ocran, have made the most substantial African contributions next to Colonel Nasser, who in many senses was a case apart.

General Ocran, writing some time after Colonel Afrifa, makes some basic statements of faith. At the start of his preface* (p. ix) he says,

Amongst the armies of British Commonwealth countries, with the exception of a few, the idea of a *coup d'état* is taboo and I believe that, if following Ghana's Independence up to the early 1960s, anyone had told me that West African Commonwealth countries would be among the exceptions, I would have doubted not only his political wisdom but also his familiarity with the traditions of armies of these countries.

This is a clear assertion of belief in what may well come to be seen as a fundamental fallacy, the a-political army. Later (p. 26) General Ocran lists the causes of Nkrumah's overthrow: it was necessary 'if Ghana was to regain her lost prestige; if she was to return to sanity; if she was not to become a base for communists; if Ghanaians were not to go hungry; if the country

* Major-General A. K. Ocran, *A Myth is Broken: An Account of the Ghana Coup d' État*, London and Accra, 1968.

was not to collapse morally and financially; in sum, if the country was not to commit national suicide.' The coup 'was not meant to give the military any privileges or special positions' (p. 27). Events seem to have justified this last assertion but the author, in writing on 'The Ghana Army Background', does stress the dangers posed by Nkrumah to the integrity and professional standards of the army through, for instance, the indoctrination of cadets in the U.S.S.R. (p. 14). He is clear that presidential interference in military affairs prepared the army for intervention in politics, albeit on behalf of the people. His criteria for the evaluation of events seem those of what is sometimes called 'a simple soldier', linking the rôle of the military patriotically with the prestige of his country. Politics scarcely comes into the book and political ideas or notions of constitutionality are barely referred to.

Colonel Afrifa's book,* though in a way it appears naïve, is nevertheless capable of more sophisticated interpretation. For those who might from harsh experience have a somewhat different view, his description of the Royal Military Academy, Sandhurst may seem to have little more than curiosity value:

> I was thrilled by Sandhurst, the beauty of its countryside, and the calm Wish Stream which separated Sandhurst from the rest of the world. Sandhurst so far was the best part of my life – learning to be a soldier in a wonderful and mysterious institution with traditions going back to 1802. . . . I met many boys of my age for whom there was nothing sweeter than bearing arms in the service of their country, boys to whom Her Majesty's Army was a symbol of their very existence. . . . I entered Sandhurst as a boy and left a soldier. There was no discrimination whatsoever. No one cared whether one was a prince, lord, commoner, foreigner, muslim or a black man. There were quite a number of lords

* Colonel A. A. Afrifa, *The Ghana Coup, 24th February 1966*, London, 1966.

and princes at Sandhurst. . . . Major Nzeogwu, reputed to have carried out the coup in Nigeria, was with us in Normandy Company (pp. 49–52).

There are, however, plenty of clues to the contrary. Essentially because Sandhurst is a British institution, Afrifa sees it as epitomizing what he regards as the virtues of British democracy, among which tolerance and a respect for constitutional behaviour are preeminent. In other words, he accepts at its face value the liberal democratic tradition. His naïvety lies in accepting to a degree uncritically the trappings of a particular institution, without recognizing the possible flaws in such a system and the undoubted difficulties involved in trying to transplant it to another society. All this, combined with the stress on professionalism, a clear understanding of the nature of allegiance and a quasi-puritanical view of man's behaviour, raises the question of the influence on the armed forces of Africa of the allegedly a-political British military tradition.

Almost certainly the a-political quality of the British as well as of other Western armies has in this context been exaggerated. It is a misleading term if what is meant is a respect for basic honesty and integrity, a well-developed sense of public duty, a concern for the national interest and a degree of impartiality in carrying out the public duty. Julius Nyerere, typically more explicit and with greater penetration than other heads of one-party states, has from time to time challenged the theory of the desirability or practicability of impartial public services of any kind in such a state. Colonel Afrifa and other Ghanaian officers apparently accepted the notion of allegiance to the government in power until in their view, and perhaps the general view, that government, in the person of Kwame Nkrumah, had passed the point where it deserved the continuance of such allegiance. For them, 'A *coup d'état* is the last resort in the range of means whereby an unpopular government may be overthrown. But in our case, where there was no constitutional means of offering a political opposition to the one-party government the Armed Forces were automatically made to become the official opposition of the government.'* There is a certain logic in this kind of switch from respect for the rule of law and the constitution to the ultimately unconstitutional action – the *coup d'état*.

But even in the case of Ghana, where a return to civilian rule has been executed, there was more than a trace not so much of a-political sentiments as of an anti-political stance. The antecedents of such thinking are not difficult to trace back to the curriculum of almost any élitist military academy where a genuine professionalism is inculcated. General de Gaulle's writings are full of reflections on the theme of the differences and the causes of antagonism between soldier and politician. The soldier's antagonism towards, and often contempt for, the politician, is virtually universal: only politicians who cultivate and respect the armed services and persuade them that they are equally identified with the national interest are immune. Thus it is probably not necessary to look as far as specifically British officer training to find an explanation for the behaviour of many of its products overseas.

It is likely, however, that the British army does not appear to the foreign trainee quite what history on the basis of experience demonstrates it to be. In the first place, explicit reference during training to the a-political character of the army is rare: the fact of non-intervention since 1688 may never be mentioned. On the other hand, individual officers clearly have and express political views, and the proper exercise of influence on policy within the framework of constitutional rules is frequently discussed. Moreover, crises like Suez and Rhodesia bring aspects of the matter from time to time to the fore. The distinction between direct political action and the constitutional exercise of influence or even pressure is a subtle one, and it may be that it is more apparent to officers from some cultural

* *Ibid.*, 31.

backgrounds than from others. It is more likely, however, that
the local socio-political situation inclines personnel one way or
another. The military élites of new states in Africa tend to be a
much more closely integrated and more substantial proportion
of the total small national leadership élite than is the case in
advanced Western countries or in India or Malaysia. In the last
two countries the forces were already largely localized before
independence and had become prestigious institutions with a
well defined rôle. In Nigeria, on the other hand, soon after
independence the political potential of the army was recognized
because of the overriding tensions and inter-regional power
struggle.

British military training does lay great stress on *esprit de
corps*. In Africa this may not always be enough to counter
other, divisive, tendencies though some would argue that it
helped, through its effect on Gowon and Ojukwu, to delay the
start of the Nigerian civil war. The sharp reaction of Ghanaian
officers to political interference in their profession could be
attributed to their British-style professionalism but in other
respects training in an alien cultural environment must create
some tensions, if not divided loyalties. No situation was more
likely to lead to the development of Afro-European cultural
hybrids than the environment of typical Western-style military
training. This was partly because of the peculiar professional
ethos and also because the physical isolation of the barracks in
a cantonment area tended to inhibit the reabsorption of
African officers into their indigenous social milieu. Moreover,
during training abroad they maintained touch with their own
people at one remove and vicariously, generally through
student organizations. But the consequent tensions experienced by individual officers were only a degree or two more
severe than those undergone by their civil service contemporaries. This situation has been well described by a number of
African novelists, notably Chinua Achebe. Personal disorientation arising from conflicting experiences in European and

African cultural environments was bound to have some effect on the political attitudes of individuals.

Whatever the other consequences of foreign military training it cannot be reasonably alleged that the European powers generally encouraged militarism. Judging by the scale of colonial defence forces, and even by the extent of recruitment to metropolitan forces in the case of France, there is no substance for this charge. After the early days of occupation the administrations were essentially civil in character. Colonial administrators like Lord Lugard, and a number of later examples, might originally have been military men or shared their general values, but there is little evidence of the militarization of society. The large recruitment during the Second World War – 228,000 from British-administered East Africa and 145,000 West Africans, for example – to some extent changed the pattern and certainly improved the socio-economic status of the successful ex-serviceman. In the towns he became the natural trustworthy concessionaire for the newly established petrol station, in the remoter areas he was often a candidate for tribal office where an element of selection or election was involved. However, though ex-servicemen played a rôle in politics, for instance in the establishment of the Convention Peoples' Party (CPP) in Ghana, it was only in certain French territories that they became a political force in themselves and this was the result of a degree of discriminatory enfranchisement. As we shall see, this may have encouraged the development of ex-military factions in French West and Equatorial Africa, but in Anglophone territories the influence of veterans was much diluted by the time of independence and evidence connecting this group and the various military coups is so far tenuous. In the British-administered areas there was no question of the discharge or redundancy of soldiers after independence, such as the French recruitment policies led to in, for example, the Togo Republic.

There has indeed generally been a considerable, though not

by any normal criteria dangerous, expansion of the armed forces since independence. But with the exception of Nigeria's army, which was inflated by the tragic circumstance of the civil war, there is scarcely a case in Africa today where the overall military complement begins to compare with the proportion of men in uniform to population in many more developed countries. On this score, then, the European colonial powers can be relieved of responsibility for the creation of overlarge military establishments and the directly attendant political consequences. Nor did they succeed in making the military overly popular as a national institution: long memories of punitive activities led to the sustenance of suspicion until well after independence in a number of cases, though the possibilities of personal advancement attracted an adequate supply of individuals to enlist. Above all, the transfer of power in Africa, with the major and significant exception of Algeria, did not involve the recruitment of a national liberation army capable of taking the place of the civil government at independence. In terms of general establishment policy and development there was, therefore, no very obvious link between the precolonial situation and the post-independence ferment.

An analysis – or even a catalogue – of those attributes which have appeared to make intervention by the military in politics practicable may, however, provoke some lines of thought about the impact of a particular national military tradition. Clearly, without arms, no army exists: they are the *sine qua non* not only of military intervention but of the existence of a military establishment. Access to a communications system separate from that available to the general public is a commonly observed asset and in this respect the peculiarly British brand of police–military relations which was introduced into colonial Africa seems to have some significance. A police radio network was in the cases of Nigeria and Ghana in 1966 an important element in the control of the situation. It seems likely that the ready accessibility of the system to army personnel may have been due to the cultivation of distinct rôles for the two services and the consequent absence of inter-service rivalries. Events in French-speaking countries have not revealed parallel ease of relationships, perhaps due to the dual rôle of the gendarmerie. The fact that the British have always been reluctant to arm their police may have some bearing on the position.

Related to the question of police–military co-operation is the clearly formulated British doctrine of the rôle of the military in aid of the civil power and the resultant emphasis placed in British military training establishments on this aspect of internal security. The U.N. Congo experience demonstrated quite clearly the superiority of the training of the forces of Commonwealth countries in this respect; indeed, the techniques of riot control were demonstrated by the Ghanaian contingent to Swedish and Irish units. Such procedures tend to institutionalize co-operation between the public services, and the apparently spontaneous success of the Ghana coup against Nkrumah might well be attributed substantially to this factor. There may, however, be a more profound effect stemming from these practices. Action in aid of the civil power has a strongly constitutional flavour and is overtly in the interests of internal stability. It may not be far-fetched to suppose that for some military leaders trained in these methods, it would be simple to rationalize military intervention in politics in circumstances where the integrity of the state appears to be threatened as an extension of the routine internal security rôle. Certainly a disciplined army with the appropriate hierarchical organization operates efficiently with the minimum of consultation partly because it has been familiarized by training to respond without question. The ready response of Kotoka's men in Ghana and of Nzeogwu's in Nigeria, when the real situation was at a late hour revealed to them, is likely to have been conditioned by this factor.

The policy, particularly marked in the British tradition, of encouraging the social separation of officers from men and the army as a whole from the civil community has also played its part. The building of cantonments, the concentration and effective organization of military wives and families – still carried on at any rate in West Africa, – and the exclusive officers' mess, have all helped to facilitate the organization of coups. The fact that the military are not accountable for their activities has meant that movements by night have gone largely unquestioned, except possibly by the police. It is indeed very hard to avoid the conclusion that the qualities of exclusiveness, discipline and cohesion, which are regarded as the virtues of a professional organization in the Western world, are in other contexts conducive to conspiracy and the plotting of a successful *coup d'état*.

The emphasis so far has been on the mechanics of intervention and the capacity to make it effective. The motivation of such action may not in fact require particularly elaborate analysis. In tropical Africa one cannot point with confidence to any case where the army appears to have seized power in order to fulfil an ideological aim or to carry out a detailed political programme. It is not in this context necessarily pejorative to imply that many of the officers involved in intervention have appeared politically naïve. This naivety could be ascribed to their simple professional values and certainly Colonel Afrifa's attitudes are capable of explanation in this way. The relationship between a general concern for national prestige and an attention to such apparent trivialities as standards of hygiene, punctuality and personal behaviour is proven. Defence forces trained in foreign traditions are a channel whereby alien notions seep into society and assist it in the process of modernization in a limited way. Once this occurs expectations are increased and images are created. It may be that those military régimes which patently fail to live up to the stereotypes which they themselves have created are the soonest vulnerable to overthrow by other insurgents.

The initial reaction of the populace to military coups in

Africa, at least in the capital cities, has frequently been one of joy and enthusiasm. This is not only accountable in terms of relief at the overthrow of régimes from which the inspirational glow of independence has faded. An impression of a just, impartial and relatively uncorrupt military man has been created by attempts to instil professional standards. When popular discontent and grievance has mounted, the emergence of such an individual or group of individuals has the dramatic effect of a *deus ex machina* even though, as in Ghana, the immediate motives may have been the protection of professional interests. Thus the alien British military tradition may be said to have worked in two directions. It must be reiterated that this does not imply any disloyalty of army officers involved to their own people, nor indeed is there implicit in the acquired attitudes any skill in political manipulation or reorientation. The reverse may well be true and the penalties for a degree of political innocence become apparent. The cultivation of an a-political – as opposed to an anti-political – viewpoint may have generated an initial reluctance to take political action: it will certainly have placed a premium on political detachment which tends to isolate the military leaders when in power and to militate against consultation. The progressive decline of military administrations is in large measure attributable to this. Officers trained by Britain have perhaps been no better and no worse than others in administering states. It may, however, be significant that in those countries, e.g. Ghana under Nkrumah, Zambia and Tanzania, which have been involved in the training of 'freedom fighters' and the promotion of guerilla operations, officers trained for the regular forces appear to have played little part. It may be that such men are more concerned with the reputation of their own state than with the subversion of their neighbours.

The armed forces of French-speaking Africa are in fact in much the same position today as their counterparts in the Commonwealth countries. As national armies they only began to emerge after independence: only the FLN in Algeria laid the foundations for a post-independence force through their fight for freedom. But in order to examine the effects of French influence on civil–military relations in West and Equatorial Africa it is necessary to take into account general and particular differences between the two former imperial powers in terms both of policy and practice. For while the British raised separate colonial forces organized regionally with units recruited in particular territories, the French attempted 'assimilation' which meant in military terms essentially the recruitment of African soldiers for the French metropolitan forces. On the face of it this clear and well defined policy should have greatly weakened the attachment of such men to their homelands by an intermingling of personnel from as far apart as Madagascar and Senegal. Moreover, it allowed for a much greater contact with European colleagues than the practice pursued by the British. In all it led to a greater loss of identity and in some cases to a virtually total severance of connections with the traditional tribal background. The rewards were a French style of life and an accompanying relative prosperity.

In the 1950s the growing awareness of imminent political change caused the French authorities to make a much more deliberate effort than the British to assimilate African military personnel by the use of training methods normally employed in France and by setting up special schools for officers and NCOs both in France and in West Africa. The intensive 'crash' courses run in these institutions paralleled British attempts to train African civil servants at, for example, the Institute of Administration at Zaria in Northern Nigeria. During the colonial period the French authorities paid much more attention than the British to the education and pre-training of children, preferably from military backgrounds. The result was that a number of those who have achieved power in French-speaking territories, such as Presidents Lamizana in Upper Volta, Bokassa in the Central African Republic and Soglo in

Dahomey, were in a real sense French officers. The most remarkable case is that of Soglo who only took Dahomeyan as opposed to French citizenship on promotion to the rank of colonel in 1961. Moreover, these men and others came to military maturity not only in some cases by service in the Second World War but through experience in Indo-China and later Algeria. The Algerian situation in particular enforced identity with and commitment to French interests in a colonial war in Africa: the nearest parallel to these cases in Anglophone territories is that of Major-General Idi Amin, who in January 1971 overthrew President Obote in Uganda and who had fought against the Mau Mau in Kenya, though not as a commissioned officer. The thorough immersion of soldiers from Francophone countries in an alien and imperial military tradition could scarcely be matched anywhere in the ex-British colonies. Colonel Alley, who eventually succeeded Soglo as President of Dahomey, was one of those who had been to a military school for children – that at Bingerville in the Ivory Coast.

When in 1958 President de Gaulle created the community of African states which included the Malagasy Republic, the intention was to provide for defence on a community basis. Thus it was not until the Community disintegrated that the nuclei of national armies were handed over by the French to the successor states. The Ivory Coast, for example, had no army of its own until the first anniversary of its independence in 1961. Perhaps because of its exceptionally close links with France, it has so far not been affected by political activity on the part of its army, but elsewhere in West and Equatorial Africa there has been adequate evidence of an inclination to independent action on the part of the military which must owe something to the French legacy.

The fact that under the French system there was no clear-cut distinction between metropolitan and overseas troops is a factor always to be borne in mind in examining not only the incidence but the nature of the coups in her former African colonies. The extensive reliance on conscripts rather than volunteers may also have been significant. Conscription was instituted in West Africa as early as 1912 and soon after was used as a bargaining counter in order to obtain concessions with regard to citizenship and the franchise. In 1916 Blaise Diagne, Senegal's first African deputy, was successful in a campaign to establish the citizenship rights of Africans while preserving their personal civil status, because of the French need to recruit large numbers of African troops for use in Europe. Similarly in 1939, the price of the expansion of the French forces was the concession of the right to vote for colonial councillors to those who had completed their military service. The result was that in Dahomey, for instance, by 1948 nearly sixty per cent of the electorate were veterans or serving soldiers. It is true that the West African territories also had to pay a financial price for the extension of electoral participation in the shape of a contribution to imperial defence expenditure even between the wars. The institutionalization of a military and ex-service rôle in politics in this way created a climate which made possible and almost natural the succession of military-dominated governments, in Dahomey in particular, from 1963 onwards.

The effect of French overseas military policy on France's relationship with the territories after independence was profound. The unwillingness to charge France with 'neo-colonialism' and to criticize her international relationships, as compared with the criticism which Britain has somewhat unfairly attracted, can be traced back in part to the developments described above. Though in the middle 1950s the most active West African political party, the Rassemblement Démocratique Africain (RDA), was vociferously opposed to the use of African troops in Algeria and at Suez, a sympathetic understanding of French interests had generally prevailed. In 1940 Equatorial Africa backed General de Gaulle strongly when France was defeated and 10,000 men served in General

Leclerc's force in North Africa. The allegiance to France cultivated in training throughout the pre-independence period seemed to override and camouflage the hostility generated by conscription, unscrupulous recruiting officers and punitive expeditions in a number of areas. British territories were at times treated as a refuge from conscription, which in some places was regarded as the equivalent of slavery. The French authorities, having raised large armies overseas, were slow to see the implications of demobilization for the territories concerned. Unrest after the Second World War was to some extent reproduced after independence in the early 1960s when the Community dissolved. It is well known that this led directly to the coup in the Togo Republic in 1963 and to the assassination of President Sylvanus Olympio, though in many ways the resentment of those concerned would have been more justly directed at the French authorities.

At each stage before independence the French had managed very effectively to redress the major grievances, and presumably obtained lasting credit by so doing. In 1948 a commission under Commandant Henri Ligier set up a complex organization to deal with veterans' affairs, guaranteeing privileges including jobs and low-cost housing. When the French subsequently withdrew from Indo-China in 1954, these arrangements were maintained to cope with a fresh batch of discharged soldiers, and although discrimination between French and African soldiers, in terms of pay and conditions, continued the essential relationships remained good. From 1950 onwards, when the Military Defence Committee of Central Africa was formed and the importance of Africa in relation to NATO began to be realized, the French attitude became more constructive and far-sighted. In particular, the speed of Africanization was accelerated by the creation of four preparatory military schools in West Africa with accommodation for five hundred African soldiers and the officer training establishment, L'École Général Leclerc, was opened in Chad.

In some senses the Sara people of Chad and their attitudes to military service reflect most clearly the effects of French influence on this aspect of African affairs. During the Indo-China war more of them volunteered than were strictly necessary and later, because they were almost entirely non-Muslim, they were not seriously influenced by Arab propaganda about participation in North Africa. At a time when political activity by Africans in both the French West and Equatorial regions was increasing, they tended to consolidate the influence of the French tradition and were to some extent recognized by the colonial authorities as a counter to political militancy organized through France-based political parties. Their rewards included the establishment in the Logone region of *villages de 15 ans* in which long-serving veterans had the chance to make a civilian life for themselves in a semi-military environment. Wounded ex-servicemen were even exempted from poll-tax. The acceptability of French support for President Tombal-baye's régime in Chad is, therefore, not surprising. Elsewhere, in what was then, in 1948, Moyen-Congo, examples could be found of African veterans rallying to the support of Gaullist RPF (Rassemblement du Peuple Français) deputies against Communist attack and the relevant mood continued to be evident in political meetings at Brazzaville and Pointe Noire up to the eve of independence.

The basis of French influence on post-independence politics in Francophone Africa is, therefore, much clearer than that of British influence in the Anglophone areas. Not only did development during the colonial period sow the seeds of a continuing pro-French orientation by slowing down or even thwarting processes which might have led to the evolution of strong indigenous institutions but it tended to identify the military element thoroughly with the imperial power, thereby giving it a political identity of its own. Moreover, large-scale recruitment and the policy for the resettlement of discharged soldiers led to a heavy reliance on military pay and veterans' pensions for the viability of the economies. The effect of this was magnified by the fragmentation of Africa into administrative-economic units such as Chad and the Central African Republic which had few resources on which to rely for development. Though, as already suggested, it would be difficult to prove the militarization of society by the French authorities in any vicious sense, there is no doubt that in a number of territories the rôle played by the military in providing the framework for civil administration and social services was fundamental. This particularly applied to medical provision, which was essentially in the hands of army doctors and which has been since independence an area where French assistance has been carried out by personnel in the course of their military service. Educationally and technically, however, the French administrations neglected, for whatever reason, the opportunity presented by conscription for literacy campaigns and the inculcation of skills. At one stage basic recruit training was of only twenty-eight days duration and was always much less than that under British auspices which never, even in wartime, fell below six months.

The rapid changes which took place during the period 1958–61 led to the somewhat abrupt transfer of African soldiers of all ranks into the charge of political leaders who were untried and from whom alienation was perhaps to be expected. The transfer of troops was generally related to the drawing up of defence agreements which involved the retention of French bases on African soil. In the majority of the eleven cases where such agreements were made, the expense of the bases was important to the economies of the territories and the programmed French withdrawal of their main military presence from Africa after 1964 had the important side effect of undermining the territories' financial position. In some cases this incidental withdrawal of an effective subsidy was conducive to creating a climate in which civil and military grievances might combine to facilitate a coup. Recognition of the political and military importance of the French connection is perhaps most clearly brought out in an incident in the Ivory Coast in September 1967 in which a joint Ivorian and French exercise was held because:

> The Ivory Coast government wanted to prove the loyalty of the army, to show it was much more concerned with protecting the country against any possible external aggression than in seeking to overthrow the government. It was also an opportunity for the Ivory Coast army to have further contact with the French army, to which many Ivorian soldiers used to belong.*

Generally speaking, English-speaking countries in Africa have not sought such opportunities, though it may be worth recording that there has been some exchange of training facilities between Ghana and Britain in recent years and that British units have trained in Kenya as well as providing assistance to the Kenya forces on the Somali border.

On the whole the conviction, so well exemplified by the career of General de Gaulle, that the army is a necessary attribute of national pride and unity has played a more positive rôle in Francophone than in Anglophone Africa, probably be cause it is more explicitly part of the French tradition. A positive, direct concern for the reputation of the nation can quickly be transformed into action aimed at instilling discipline in the young and protecting a code of moral values. There is no need to go further than this for an explanation of such decrees by military régimes as those issued at different times in the Voltaic Republic prohibiting drum-playing and lying about in the sun except on Sundays and the wearing of miniskirts except for sporting purposes. The French administrations in West and Equatorial Africa had created institutions which ensured the continuing importance of the military for economic and social

* Guy de Lusignan, *French-Speaking Africa since Independence*, London, 1969, 357.

development and their step by step entrenchment in a key rôle in national life. It was not to be expected that men who had been of some significance in the armed forces of a major world power would be content with a miniscule rôle guarding frontiers which were generally not threatened on behalf of politicians whom they often came quickly to despise. Matters were perhaps most likely to come to a head over recruitment policies. For, like the British, the French had for sound imperial reasons relied generally on soldiers from selected areas of the hinterland who could be relied on for loyalty or neutrality, according to the viewpoint, in dealing with dissidence amongst the urban dwellers and the inhabitants of the coastal areas. Mass political support was, however, often derived from these very areas and some readjustment of the balance of manpower within armed forces was a reasonable political expectation.

It is therefore perhaps especially in Francophone areas, where the association of military units with particular colonial territories was not traditional, that one should look for political activity by the military in which intergenerational tensions play a part. The distinction between those who had been recruited for the French forces before independence and those raised at political behest for the indigenous national army after independence was a potential source of fission which ambitious politicians would scarcely ignore. The relative success of a number of French-trained African officers in establishing military régimes may well have been due to their subconscious emulation of General de Gaulle, and if this is so then the imperial military legacy must be regarded as a significant factor in the interpretation of military intervention in politics, at any rate for the time being.

The problem remains to indicate other possible connections between the military traditions of imperial powers and the behaviour of their inheritors in new African states. In attempting so to do, a distinction between the factors conducive to the execution of a coup and those leading to the consolidation and

continuance of a military régime is important. First it is necessary to exclude events which properly fall into the category of
a 'mutiny'. The *Force Publique* mutinied in the Congo in 1960
but the reconstituted national army under Mobutu effectively
staged a coup in 1965. The events in East Africa in January
1964 in Tanganyika, Uganda and Kenya were essentially
mutinies. A mutiny may be described as military unrest arising
from grievances about conditions, pay, promotions and localization or Africanization policy – about matters, that is to say,
which are essentially if not completely internal to the defence
force concerned. A mutiny, unlike a coup, has not an immediate
political objective, though if it is prolonged it is quite likely
that it will acquire one and in so doing change its nature. This
is not, of course, to say that involvement in mutiny may not
give military personnel a taste for political power: in fact this
is the prime reason for regarding the ultimate disbandment of
mutinous units as politically prudent for the state in question.
In any case an uncertain reaction by a government to a mutiny
in its army encourages political awareness and an appreciation
of the potential of direct intervention. For instance, Idi Amin,
when a major in 1964, used his ability to inhibit the malcon-
tents at Jinja barracks from violent action to extract from the
Prime Minister, Milton Obote, the promise of pay rises and
immediate Africanization of key posts. His intervention
brought that particular mutiny to an end. His subsequent relations with Obote, culminating in the seizure of power in
January 1971, illustrate this point well and will be referred to
more fully.

The legacy of the colonial powers to Africa, judging by the
experience of Britain and France, is compounded of two main
elements. In the first place there is the general Western military
professional ethos, which is directly or indirectly inculcated
through training establishments or by the loan of personnel.
This may be made up of a set of intangible values and the
methods and content of the training and educational process.

Of particular importance may be the political climate or more especially the revealed attitudes to the constitution, law and politicians. Secondly, there are the consequences, not often thought out or foreseen, of policies which were adopted during the colonial period and which reflect either the style of imperial rule or its fulfilment of strategic or other needs on the basis of expediency. In this connection, for example, the French policy of assimilation which involved the enlistment of African personnel for service in the metropolitan army is important, especially when contrasted with the British method; so is the convention, adopted by both powers for similar reasons, of recruitment from the less educated and politically conscious peoples of the hinterland. Other important elements are clearly the extent of recruitment during the world wars and to fight colonial wars elsewhere in peace time and the extent of internal security commitments within particular territories during the run-up to independence. It has frequently been suggested that the use of armies in a police rôle on a recurrent basis encourages the development of a propensity to intervene politically. In fact, however, a feature of the last thirty years of colonial history in Africa is the relative peace which prevailed and which gave time for memories of initial conquest and punitive expeditions to fade. In British-administered territories in particular the normal reluctance to deploy the army was reinforced by the absence of critical occasions in which to do so, except notably for the Mau Mau emergency in Kenya.

Discussion of these aspects of the transferred tradition in the end seems to focus on the question whether the political ideology of the colonial power has rubbed off in a lasting way on to its former military protégés. As we have seen, the answer appears to be that what is transferred is obliquely rather than directly related to the political orientation of the imperial power and that an immediate doctrinaire purpose is not a normal characteristic of African coup leaders. It may indeed be much more important to take into account the length of

preparation for independence, and the degree of Africanization
of the officer corps at the time of its achievement and the subsequent speed of the process as well as the extent of expansion
of the armed forces as a whole. At this point the continuance of
tutelage by the imperial power or alternatively the extent of
the diversification of military assistance are relevant as well as
opportunities for the gaining of military experience and, therefore, of confidence as a result of an operational commitment.

The possible application of some of these criteria may perhaps best be judged by a brief comparison of the circumstances
in which the armies of Ghana in February 1966 and Uganda in
January 1971 respectively deposed their Presidents, Nkrumah
and Obote, *in absentia* as it were. In both cases the Presidents
had established one-party régimes internally and developed
pan-Africanist aspirations reflected in foreign policies towards
Communist and ex-imperial powers in obvious ways. Both
forces had had some substantial military experience – the
Ghana force in the Congo and the Uganda army on the Sudanese and Congolese borders. In each case there had been some
interference with the army command by the President which
had been resented by some elements within the force. In each
case Communist military assistance had been sought and a
private army assembled around the President. Here, however,
the main similarities, however important they may seem, end.

The Ghana army had African officers commissioned nearly
ten years before independence and by that date had a reasonable number of well-educated men in the military hierarchy.
The Uganda army at independence had precisely nine African
officers all commissioned in the preceding eighteen months and
with one exception from the ranks of senior serving soldiers.
The mutiny of 1964 in Uganda revealed the lack of an established professionalism such as was displayed by most Ghanaian
units in the Congo in 1960. The Uganda army, led by General
Amin, had allowed itself perforce to be used for a factional
political purpose against the Baganda and, in particular, in the

attack on the Kabaka's palace. The Ghana army had been markedly reluctant to be used as a political tool in face of a serious strike in 1962 and was relatively cohesive and not rent by major tribal divisions; whereas in Uganda the Acholi and Lango dominance in certain units was encouraged by the President apparently to consolidate his own political power base. According to observers there has been little comparison between the two forces in the matter of discipline and the attitude to foreigners.

There is, therefore, a strong superficial similarity between the two countries in the matter of the occasion of a coup, but in the case of Uganda there is no indication of the reluctance born of great military maturity which was a feature of the Ghana army's relatively non-violent intervention, and so far there is no great evidence of the capacity to inspire confidence in the population as a whole which seems to be a function of the professional image, as shown by the Ghana case. It is not difficult to predict that any attempts to return to civil rule in Uganda will have a different outcome from Ghana. The employment of similar criteria relating to the establishment of an experienced officer corps and the continuance of a connection with the parent ex-imperial army might be held to explain the way in which Uganda has succumbed to the military as compared with President Kenyatta's skilful avoidance of military intervention in neighbouring Kenya. The rapid expansion of the Uganda army after 1964 must be regarded as another important variable tending to lead to an unstable situation.

If one turns to military régimes which have successfully survived for a period the strains of exercising authority, it is observable that the important factors are those which seem to have enabled the Ghana army to execute a plan for a return to civilian rule. It may be said of the military in Nigeria and General Mobutu in Zaire that they continue in office because for the most part they have appeared to live up to the expectations created by a military régime. Their professionalism has been paramount, they have apparently exercised a moderating influence, and have not been unduly partial nor appeared overtly and grossly corrupt. In other words, they have identified themselves for the time being with the apparent national interest and have attempted to achieve a measure of efficiency. They have succeeded rightly or wrongly in presenting an acceptable image and they owe this in large measure to having adopted techniques and methods consistent with a received but alien set of values. At least this is a possible explanation from the military standpoint of their degree of success. Similarly, the failure of Brigadier Juxon-Smith in Sierra Leone can be explained by his inability from the first to carry out the rôle to which he succeeded in accordance with any recognizable norms. He antagonized his military colleagues, the senior civil servants and the police. His arbitrary behaviour suggested a perverse enjoyment of power for its own sake and his commitment to a return to civilian rule was patently insincere. He and the National Reformation Council under his chairmanship made no attempt to clean up corruption or to cope with diamond smuggling and its consequences. Tribal influences were allowed to predominate and there was no evidence in the circumstances of the coup of a true concern for the national interest.

Hence it may be said that the kind of military régimes which are likely to achieve power in Africa on the basis of personnel trained in Europe or by Western Europeans owe their opportunities to a bequeathed professionalism. Their reluctance to engage in unconstitutional action, their style in engaging in it and the success of their subsequent administration all seem to depend on the depth of the professional veneer which itself is influenced by the multiplicity of factors described. The responsibility of justifying in practice the widespread stereotyped reputation of the professional soldier educated in an appropriate mould is often too much for those who aspire to it.

An analysis of the peculiar military contribution to the state of political flux prevailing in contemporary Africa must, however, take into account other more general factors. Not only did the colonial powers leave behind in many cases an inadequately developed military professionalism. They also, through circumstances at the end not entirely within their control, left behind little foundation for government by consent. This was barely practicable in a situation involving mass poverty and an acutely uneven distribution of wealth. The military, possessing arms, have seemed on many occasions to be the natural alternative to the disintegration of the state in the face of ethnic and other divisions even within a ruling oligarchy. In such conditions political power may well be the only means to real wealth, and employment for the educated élite, in particular, may depend almost wholly on the patronage of those individuals who currently have that power. There is therefore nothing surprising about the exercise of political judgment by the one-time colonial defence forces of Africa. They are simply demonstrating what has been termed 'the principle of the naturalness of despotism'. The concentration of study and analysis should, therefore, perhaps be on the non-occurrence of military intervention rather than on the matters which provoke it. The timing of recent coups is in large measure explicable in terms of the factors affecting the conversion of colonial defence forces into national armies. The continuing problem is the analysis of the whole range of civil military relations in Africa as the continent's military establishments begin to move slowly out of this transitional phase in their development. The recurrent phenomenon of military intervention in politics is already, almost by definition as it were, of less significance than the performance of the military in government.

III · Military Rule in Ghana

Though the Ghana army had, as it were, marched back to barracks in September 1969, the dissolution of the interim Presidential Commission in August 1970 formally affirmed the re-establishment of civilian rule. On that occasion General A. A. Afrifa, who had for a brief period in 1968–9 been head of state, confidently asserted, 'Now that our rifles are down, they are down for ever.' In less than eighteen months, on 13 January 1972, a new military régime was set up under the leadership of Colonel I. K. Acheampong and justified its displacement of Dr Kofi Busia's administration on much the same grounds as Afrifa and his colleagues had used in overthrowing Kwame Nkrumah in February 1966. Afrifa himself was subsequently detained by his military successors and must on many occasions have recalled his own 'crisis of conscience' in helping to engineer the earlier coup, and perhaps also President Nkrumah's address to the cadets of the Ghana Military Academy at Teshie in May 1961, when he emphasized that 'It is not the duty of a soldier to criticize or endeavour to interfere in any way with the political affairs of the country.'

The performance of the military in government in Ghana is properly seen as part of a continuum and not as two isolated episodes, one of which at the time of writing shows signs of relative permanency. It is not only that Acheampong appeared from the first to have learnt from and built on the experience of Ankrah and Afrifa but that both régimes were inevitably conditioned by the manner in which they achieved power and generally by the succession of expectations and disappointments since independence. In a sense the sequence of events in Ghana seems less arbitrary than in other cases. From the stand-

point of 1974 it seemed almost as though for twenty years the
country had been following a predetermined course, providing
a classic illustration of the problems implicit in the evolution of
a post-colonial political system and a commentary on the whole
question of the military in politics.

As early as December 1972 the apparent success, in economic
terms, of Colonel Acheampong's administration was being regarded in some quarters as a proper conclusion to what had
gone before: it was as though the high hopes for Ghanaian
development euphorically engendered by the champions of
colonial independence in the 1950s were at last being realized.
Here, it appeared, was a government which had emerged from
its first year of office with a better record in, for example,
agricultural development than most others in West Africa. The
international indebtedness of Ghana had actually been reduced
during the period in question and the régime's protagonists
could claim, with some justice, that it was not more repressive
or illiberal than its democratically elected predecessor. A long
forgotten and differently directed optimism seemed to be in the
process of vindication and military rule seemed almost respectable.

On the other hand, the forceful, though bloodless, overthrow
of Dr Busia's government had engendered a traumatic sense of
finality within and outside Africa. On the face of it, the displacement by military intervention of an administration which
had come to power only a relatively short time before as the
result of what was admittedly the best conducted and most
democratic election ever held in post-independence tropical
Africa was hard to justify. Disappointing though Dr Busia's
record in office may have been, the legitimacy of his government could scarcely be challenged. Colonel Acheampong's
seizure of power had demonstrated that henceforward no régime
in West Africa was safe from military action: any government
might be overthrown at any time, whatever its record and its
democratic credentials. Moreover, participants in civilian

governments and those like General Afrifa who appeared to have given them genuine and disinterested support were likely to be at risk of imprisonment and deprivation of their rights and property. Within the short span of three years groups within the Ghanaian élite had pioneered the route back from military to civilian rule and then resoundingly demonstrated the almost total irrelevance of the exercise.

An obstacle to the understanding of the Ghanaian experience and of others similarly involving a mélange of representative institutions, life presidents, a one-party state, the restraint of opposition, control of the press and the advent of the army as a kind of *deus ex machina*, is clearly the widespread assumption (or delusion?) that the norm consists of some form of parliamentary democracy, while military rule is a deviant abnormality. Whatever the emotional basis for the world-wide abhorrence of military régimes, the fact is that in this century the majority of states – even those well established by 1917 – have experienced military rule in one form or another. The Ghanaian case provides a valuable opportunity for testing the claim that the army, in the exercise of political power, is often more liberal than a one-party or even a multi-party civilian government, and also for assessing the more obviously disputable assertion that it has some capacity to reform polity and society and to further the evolution of a broad-based and therefore presumably more stable political system. The importance of the paradoxical Ghanaian experience lies in the extent to which through its apparent contradictions it illuminates these questions. As a case study it also has the humane merit that the succession of régimes has taken place with less violence and on the whole more limited repression and even personal hardship than in most parallel cases. This may or may not be attributable to peculiarly Ghanaian characteristics.

On the whole, the last ten years in Africa have tended to substantiate Professor Finer's* original suggestion that mili-

* In *The Man on Horseback*, London, Pall Mall Press, 1962.

tary initiatives in politics are most often the product of a low
level of political culture in circumstances where there has been
virtually inevitable economic disappointment, compounded by
financial mismanagement. The term 'praetorianism', implying
the emergence of the military as an independent political force,
has only limited validity when applied to Sub-Saharan Africa.
The tendency, well illustrated in Ghana, has been for military
action to reflect a convergence of military with civilian discontent and for military régimes to be based on the same
institutional and personal infrastructure as their civilian predecessors. The military leadership in a small country like Ghana
is essentially an integral part of a relatively small national élite
in which close family and educational connections cut across
the whole range of professional and managerial occupations. In
Ghana in 1960 there was perhaps, in sociological terms, a clear
distinction between the composition of the leadership of the
Convention People's Party (CPP) and the educated élite, but
the emergent officer class was unequivocally part of the latter.

The fact that the whole élite was, and indeed still largely is,
part of the distinctive legacy of colonial rule is of considerable
significance for the style of military administrations. Whatever
their composition their external reference group in sociological
terms remains for the time being the same. Ghana's military
officer corps was educated and trained in the ethos of British
professionalism. Only now, towards the mid-seventies and
nearly twenty years after independence, are names unfamiliar
to the imperial mentors beginning to appear in key rôles.
Colonel Acheampong's coup saw the emergence of a new group
of military administrators but they were still men who had been
trained in Britain or by the British in the 1950s and early
1960s. This long continuation of the colonial link has only
applied in a few cases in Nigeria, partly because of the decima-
tion of the original cadre by the coups and the civil war, and for
different reasons hardly at all in Uganda. Appreciation of the
distinction between civil political activity and military respon-

sibility was in fact greatly reinforced by the duties which colonial defence forces were called upon to perform. Though they served overseas in the two world wars, there was no prevalent conception at independence of an international rôle: the army was there to patrol the frontiers and, if necessary, to aid the civil power, which had, of course, until very recently been essentially foreign and not national. Rigorous selection procedures and training inculcated – no doubt subconsciously and largely accidentally – not so much an a-political as an anti-political professionalism. Only at the last minute of colonial rule was responsibility for defence and security transferred to African hands and even then expatriate soldiers and policemen remained for some time the immediate agents of authority. Local military personnel had not and could not in these circumstances have played any active part in the achievement of independence: their only rôle indeed was to help the imperial power in controlling the uglier and more violent elements of the process. There was thus widespread ignorance of the nature and purpose of armed forces: in Ghana Kwame Nkrumah and his political colleagues had no direct acquaintance or experience with them, except in so far as they relied to some extent on the support of ex-servicemen. The armed services, therefore, only slowly became national institutions, but probably benefited by acquiring in the process a politically advantageous reputation for detachment and concern for the public good.

By 1960 and the declaration of Nkrumah as the President of the Republic of Ghana, a military tradition could be said to have been relatively easily and early established. In spite of increasing discontent with the Nkrumah régime in some quarters, notably the higher ranks of the civil service, the army leadership, under the guidance of General Alexander, acquiesced in the precipitate decision by the President to intervene in the Congo in July/August 1960. This was, however, a turning point in Kwame Nkrumah's relationship with the army because the Congo embroilment focused attention on two of the main issues which since that time have most concerned the Ghanaian military in and out of power – namely their own professional integrity and the international reputation of their government. Their disquiet on these two scores can be traced back to the machinations of the Ghanaian ambassadors in Leopoldville, A. Djin and N. A. Welbeck, and to the instructions of the President which appeared from time to time to be at variance with the professional responsibility of the Ghanaian contingent to the UN command. The undoubted strain of operations in the international limelight created foci of inflammation which enlarged over the years as the régime became more fearful and oppressive. For at least two further years, however, a fairly systematic attempt was made by Nkrumah to cultivate the military through banquets, other entertainments and generally privileged treatment.

At first the nationalist drive for localization of the officer corps had been blunted by Nkrumah's own politically astute reluctance, but for a variety of reasons, including pan-African reactions and Russian influence, the situation was later transformed by the dismissal of the British general, H. T. Alexander, in September 1961. There followed a series of measures which were actually or apparently a threat to the integrity of the armed forces. The Granville Sharp Commission of inquiry into the alleged plot against Nkrumah had been sufficient to alert perceptive army officers of the danger of involvement in extra-military affairs which might be interpreted in political terms.

The extent to which the shift in the President's constitutional position *vis-à-vis* the armed forces, embodied in the revised Ghana constitution of 1960, was fundamental to the deterioration of relations between the President and the military must remain a moot point. Certainly the President's position was entrenched in a number of ways. Effectively only the size and the formal initiative for raising armed forces remained with Parliament. The President could dismiss or suspend military personnel or exercise a veto on an officer's authority without consultation. He could commit the defence forces to operations for a number of specific reasons or for 'any other expedient purpose' and in effect had the personal authority to determine a state of war without prior parliamentary approval. He was, as Supreme Commander, *ex-officio* Chairman of the Defence Committee and of the Chiefs of Staff Committee. He could authorize the commissioning of officers and they must swear allegiance to him. The opportunity available to him to prefer particular officers and thereby to commit sections of the army to a political cause was clear. The army could be involved in foreign adventures in anticipation of parliamentary approval which, in any case, was not likely to be difficult to obtain in a one-party state. The attribution of subsequent arbitrary actions to the existence of these powers and growing suspicion about the President's future intentions seem to have contributed substantially to the change of officer attitudes which eventually made the 1966 coup possible.

The Ghana army contrived, in spite of all the difficulties, to emerge from the Congo crisis with public and international credit and with a growing confidence in itself as a professional body. The officers realized the favourable comparisons drawn between their own contingents and those from a number of other African countries, and they were proud of having been able to demonstrate some of their special skills in internal security to European neutrals such as Sweden and Ireland: their distrust of politicians had been enhanced not only by their own ambassadorial representatives in Leopoldville, but by the anarchic state of the Congolese government. The total effect of the experience on the army was summed up effectively in a single sentence in Colonel A. A. Afrifa's book *The Ghana Coup, 24th February 1966* (p. 66) – 'Could it be that we had been sent to the Congo to foster the ambition of Kwame Nkrumah?' The murder of Ghanaian soldiers by the Congolese at Port Francqui was attributed to political foolhardiness and thereafter, the possibility of commitment to some patently disastrous course, such as a single-handed expedition against Rhodesia, however fantastic, weighed heavily on imaginative professional minds.

In more ways than one, 1961 was a watershed in relationships between the military and political establishments. The circumstances of the dismissal of eighty British officers, including General Alexander, on 22 September 1961 were significant. The coincidence of the use of the army in the Sekondi-Takoradi strike and Nkrumah's increasing confidence about the merits of Communist military assistance seem to have led the President to this drastic but in the end inevitable decision. He felt that expatriates would be an undesirable complication if the need arose to take forceful action in the event of domestic disorder, and their known and natural opposition on political and professional grounds to sending substantial numbers of cadets to the Soviet Union for training was understandable. In the long term, the President's decision to send cadets to the Soviet Union was of more importance than his dismissal of British officers, as some at least of the African army hierarchy openly opposed the Russian arrangement. The fear that the army would be divided into rival officer cliques trained in different traditions was never realized: the target of four hundred cadets for Moscow was never achieved and of the sixty-eight who did eventually make the journey Major-General Albert Ocran wrote:

> The Ghana Armed Forces, of course, found no use for the ex-U.S.S.R. cadets on their return home. . . . There was the fear of the results of the indoctrination of the cadets. . . . The saying that 'East is East and West is West and never the twain shall meet' came to acquire a new and more vivid meaning for me when Nkrumah took his leftward turn and tried to drag the country and the Army with him.*

To this extent at least we can discern the emergence of ideo-

* Major-General A. K. Ocran, *A Myth is Broken: An Account of the Ghana Coup d'État*, London and Accra, 1968, 15.

logical differences between Kwame Nkrumah and his army, which are obviously substantially attributable to the source and style of officer training. The facts that Canadians took over the officer training rôle in Ghana from the British, that cadets continued to be sent to Sandhurst in small numbers and that by mid-1962 a two hundred strong British Joint Services Training Team had arrived did not eliminate the memory of this episode.

Within a year an assassination attempt on the President at Kulungugu in northern Ghana and an explosion at Flagstaff House, Accra, had caused the President to take new steps for his own protection involving the development of the President's Own Guard Regiment (POGR), the training of which was in the hands of East European advisers. It was given lavish Soviet equipment and, most significantly, was outside the regular chain of command. Moreover, the military and police security services were reorganized in such a way as to make them responsible directly to Nkrumah, again bypassing the channels of political responsibility. This system, combined with a comprehensive attempt to establish the ruling political party within the armed forces, made the army's leadership directly aware of the threat posed to their professionalism and to the institution's integrity. The realization that there might be 'spies in the mess', especially of other rank origin, was calculated to alarm faithful adherents of the British officer tradition more than any other single development.

Further evidence of the President's determination to subordinate the security services fully to his personal control was provided by the purge of the upper echelons of the police hierarchy in 1964 following another assassination attempt, this time by a policeman at Flagstaff House. This was followed in 1965 by the enforced retirement of the two highest ranking army officers, S. J. A. Otu and J. A. Ankrah. According to Afrifa the latter's dismissal, in particular, was deeply resented, however plausible and basically justifiable the reasons given. In informed military circles this act was seen as a substitution of political commitment for professional competence as the criterion for appointment. The threats to the unity of the armed forces, which had been made clear by the attempt to insist on CPP membership, had now reached the point where the possibility of effective resistance to interference had begun to diminish and might eventually disappear. The POGR was now more than a thousand strong and proportionately much better supplied than the army which was suffering from an acute shortage of clothing and equipment, and there were now plans to militarize the Workers' Brigade along predictable lines.

When such an accumulation of military grievances is seen in the context of economic decline and political repression it seems surprising in retrospect that no coup was attempted earlier. There is, however, no evidence that anything much more substantial than private conversations between a couple of individuals took place before the effective conspiracy. This could be attributed to a lack of courage on the part of Ghana's officer corps, but the two books by Afrifa and Ocran suggest that they, and presumably many of their colleagues, were so imbued with democratic constitutionalism that the ultimately unconstitutional act of a coup involved for them a real crisis of conscience. It would be easy to dismiss their faith in the traditions, which they seem to have acquired in Britain, as naïve, exaggerated and indeed misconceived. On the other hand, it is worth noting that in the Ghana officer corps in the post-independence/pre-coup period observers were unable to uncover examples of that aggressive anti-British xenophobia which could be found in pockets of the Nigerian army at the corresponding period. In Ghana, more than in any other case of military intervention in politics, the consequences of attempting to emulate a foreign organizational model and its accompanying ethos in a radically different social environment were highlighted.

Consideration of this important question and its effect on the subsequent behaviour of the military-police régime is complicated by the assumptions which are conventionally made about the nature of military institutions in developing countries. Notions of ideological cohesiveness, high levels of management skill, a puritanical approach to efficiency and the public good, and an especial patriotic fervour are, it must be said, all inferred as the natural consequences of transferring the military traditions of Europe to Africa. To assume that there will not be at least some distortion in the process of transfer is patently unsound. At its simplest level, it is commonly claimed that the military are orientated to the goal of modernization with the implication, amongst other things, that they have special technological skills. But it is a fact that the armed forces of tropical Africa have little in the way of trained manpower resources of this kind, for it was years after independence that the first Ghanaian army officer successfully completed the basic British technical officers' course at the Royal Military College of Science, Shrivenham. Moreover, in Britain – as indeed in France – young African officers have been trained as though they were candidates for commissions in the host country without any distinction or discrimination. Success has been judged in terms of conformity to alien norms: at Sandhurst, for example, for an African cadet such as Yakubu Gowon to become a cadet under-officer, or perhaps to represent the Academy at some sport or athletic event, was considered a remarkable achievement. Though some cadets would react, on racial or nationalist grounds, against the alien values, the majority tended to conform, primarily because of the élite status thereby to be acquired at home. Their own perception of the experience undergone was, however, likely to involve distortion or some measure of idealization.

In Ghana's case it is inevitable that heavy reliance should be placed on the testimony of Afrifa and Ocran in their books on the 1966 coup. Colonel Afrifa's effusively-expressed admiration for Sandhurst is readily understandable if one allows for a large measure of nostalgic hindsight. What is thought to be more significant is the consistently unfavourable comparison in his and General Ocran's books between the behaviour of the original Ghana nationalist movement and that of the British. The imperial power is shown as bowing more or less gracefully to the wish of the majority of the people, as being 'duty conscious' and trying 'to do that which was right against all odds'; while Nkrumah is a demagogue with a 'majority of illiterate followers' who 'disregarded brain and wisdom in favour of brawn'.* Though Afrifa was not trained at Sandhurst until after Ghana achieved independence, he had by 1966 a thorough contempt for the leaders of the independence movement in his own country. His antipathy to Nkrumah was already well developed as a cadet in 1959 and substantially due to his Ashanti origins. His basic attitudes were more certainly attributable to his origins than to any imperialist conspiracy to indoctrinate young African officers. His experience at Sandhurst, however, seems to have enabled him even more thoroughly to rationalize his decision to be involved in the overthrow of Nkrumah. 'I knew personally,' he wrote, 'that Her Majesty's Government of the United Kingdom was quite capable of dealing with the Rhodesia situation. I felt that Nkrumah was making too much noise about the whole issue.'†

> Organization of African Unity or no Organization of African Unity, I will claim my citizenship of Ghana and of the Commonwealth in any part of the world. I have been trained in the United Kingdom as a soldier, and I am ever prepared to fight alongside my friends in the United Kingdom in the same way as Canadians and Australians will do.‡

Major-General Ocran, in his justification of the action against Nkrumah, reduced the argument to the lower level of military allowances, privileges and social amenities. He enumerated the

---

* Afrifa, *op. cit.*, 54.
† *Ibid.*, 104.
‡ *Ibid.*, 112.

advantages enjoyed by members of the services in Britain and the gradual erosion of the position in Ghana: 'One day they (the military) were to pay for electricity; the next day they were to lose their training allowances; the following day, they were to lose their travelling facilities.' He added emphatically, 'We all wondered what was happening to us. . . . When the British were here our interests were better protected.'* He claimed that by 1965 army rates of pay were worth only one-third of their value in 1957.

The convergence of military and civil grounds for discontent is at this point quite clear. It must, however, be borne in mind that the criteria for officer grievances based on British norms were external to Ghana; the same might be held to apply to the whole élite who draw salaries based on scales derived originally from those applicable to expatriates and remote from the general levels of income prevailing in a less developed country. Inability to adjust the resulting wide differentials was found to affect the ability of a military régime realistically to advocate austerity. It is in this inadvertent sense rather than in terms of political conspiracy and the application of secret service funds that foreign influence on the Ghana coup against Nkrumah should probably be seen. It may also help to account for the relative lack of success of the military government and its similarly oriented civilian successor in tackling the fundamental economic problems. What remains unquestionable, even if the army acted as much in its own as in the public interest, is the genuine enthusiasm generated in the first instance amongst the mass of the people by the action of the military in February 1966. In the execution of the plan the legitimate qualms of a few soldiers and the resistance of the POGR contingent at Flagstaff House, the President's residence, were the only serious obstacles encountered: otherwise the event seemed only to serve to release the widespread popular indignation which existed against the CPP.

* Ocran, *op. cit.*, 43.

Though the ruling party had won successive elections before independence it had never been by any overwhelming margin of the national vote. It is questionable how effective a political force the CPP had ever been in the country. The heroic, in Ghanaian and more especially pan-African terms, image of Nkrumah had been sufficiently appreciated in the main centres of population in Southern Ghana to give his government authority. Though by the standards of the seventies his régime was never violently repressive, it had maintained power by an enforced consensus now broken at a blow by the military.

Sophisticated analysis of the degree of economic stagnation, of the extent of corruption, of the denial of political expression is not necessary to explain the welcome given to the National Liberation Council in 1966. The story of Ghana's economic decline between 1959 and 1964 is well attested. External trade figures remained fairly static partly due to the slump in the world prices of primary products, especially cocoa. At the same time a reserve of about $550 million derived from the pre-independence cocoa boom was transformed into a massive international debt amounting to at least half that figure. That this was due to excessive state spending on prestige projects or political expedients, reflected in almost continuous budget deficits, is well known. The results were inflation, particularly marked in 1965, and abortive measures to deal with it embodied in austerity budgets. The consequent shortages affected the ordinary consumer directly, and attempts at restriction and control increased the scope for personal enrichment of party officials through corruption in, for example, the dispensation of import licences. Such abuses affected all sections of the population and made them potentially receptive to the idea of change – perhaps any change.

The weak popular base of the CPP – only 57 per cent of the electorate even in 1955 – and the elimination of political opposition by the use of the Emergency Powers and Preventive

Detention Acts based on British wartime legislation were, how-ever, mainly matters of concern for the élite groups. The civil service, the judiciary and senior personnel in national enter-prises had become increasingly insecure as their autonomy was undermined by direct and arbitrary political interference. It was as natural that they should look to the army and the police for their salvation as that the military should take steps at the eleventh hour to preserve their corporate integrity and, as they saw it, uphold or restore the reputation of the state of Ghana in the eyes of the world.

On 24 February 1966 certain senior personnel from the mili-tary and police cadres assumed responsibility for the govern-ment of Ghana. In accordance with the generality of military régimes, they did so without any precise programme in mind: a hazy idealism, faithfully reflected in the writings of Afrifa and Ocran, and a general desire to cleanse the state from the adverse consequences of Nkrumah's presidency and to put Ghana back on course towards becoming a modern, by which may be assumed Westernized, state. Whatever long-term economic ideology may have been in the backs of the coup leaders' minds, they were immediately involved, as was their successor, Dr Busia, in tackling the urgent problems arising from an adverse balance of payments, shortage of foreign currency reserves and a negligible growth rate. They had also to justify their assump-tion of power in political terms by demonstrating, through purges of corrupt elements, the follies and vices of the previous régime. Ocran referred to 'the plunder of the public treasury and the conspicuous wealth of Nkrumah, his Ministers and Party activists' as sufficient justification for the coup.* It would be necessary to demonstrate the army's motivation in these terms in order to avoid the charge that power had been seized for the satisfaction of selfish sectional interests and that nothing had really changed. One might quote the title of a gramophone record published in Ghana in 1968 and then

* *Ibid.*, 6.

banned: 'The Cars are the Same, Only the Drivers are Different.'

The well-meaning (a term advisedly used) attempts by the National Liberation Council to reform Ghana and to steer her economy into calmer waters encountered heavy weather. The root of the difficulties lay in the lack of clear objectives. The advantages of the military as a separate and specially respected organization were not capitalized, because without a real sense of direction and ready-made links with influential elements uncontaminated by association with the old régime, its leaders unsuspectingly made *ad hoc* alliances which inhibited the possibility of a fresh start. Some informed opinion in Ghana consistently opposed to Nkrumah felt that the crucial error was the thoroughgoing alliance with the police; it was suggested that the latter represented the kinds of petty oppression and corruption of which the ordinary man or woman had the most direct experience. This was a theme which the exiled Nkrumah and his propagandists sought to exploit. To have two ex-Special Branch Senior Officers as members of the NLC did involve the risk of such allegations. It also involved, as it turned out, considerable scope for tension between the two services as well as an inhibition on major reforms in an area in which they were perhaps especially needed. The cohesion of the NLC itself was also affected by this alliance and the extreme view would be to regard the police as an albatross which the army had hung round its own neck.

There were other inherent problems of a kind which military régimes elsewhere almost inevitably have to face. Where the charges against the displaced civilian régime include extravagance and general overspending of public funds and at the same time the armed forces' equipment and privileges are run down, there is a clear dilemma. Increased defence expenditure cannot be justified as part of an austerity programme, and yet without it the credibility of the new régime's leaders with their own power base will be weakened. At the same time the fruits

of office for the oligarchy are part of the apparently essential
paraphernalia of power. A report in the Ghana *Daily Graphic* of
10 June 1968 concisely and probably unwittingly makes this
point in describing a public ceremonial in Northern Ghana:
'Air Marshal Otu and General Ocran came in black Mercedes
330s, driven by equally gorgeously uniformed soldiers. At precisely 9 o'clock General Ankrah arrived in a sleekly stream-
lined Rolls-Royce adorned with Ghana's Coat-of-Arms.'

It is not surprising that in many ways the NLC's period of
office was characterized by stagnation. A more positive rôle
would have destroyed the army's own *raison d'être* and, in any
case, the act of involvement in politics was a contradiction of
the essential tenets of belief of the 'simple' soldiers at the pin-
nacle of power. For them an early return to civilian rule was the
only way of reconciling their behaviour with their deeply
imbued professionalism. In the interim their political conduct
was simplistic: they endeavoured to consolidate the popularity
which they had achieved by the overthrow of Nkrumah by
courting sectional interests which had been forced into opposition by denial of their status and basic rights. The chiefs re-
covered their lost power and prestige, private businessmen were
allowed more scope for their commercial operations and the in-
tellectuals – the university academics – regained in a large
measure their freedom of expression. Though the abortive but
nearly successful counter-coup of April 1967 showed that there
were grave loopholes in the security arrangements, the NLC
quickly acquired the capacity for political survival. The emphasis must be on the word 'survival' for the régime failed to
develop a positive dynamic: its reasons for taking power had
been, as has been demonstrated, largely negative. The implementation of the necessary administrative measures was only
practicable if the existing civil service structure was harnessed
to NLC ends.

During its reign the National Liberation Council presided
over an essentially civilian structure: officers of the armed

forces filled only a limited number of ministerial and top regional administrative posts. Apart from those like Major-General Nathan Aferi who were appointed ambassadors or high commissioners, the total of those employed in extra-military rôles rarely exceeded twelve in all. The permanent civil service came back into its own and effectively ran the ministries; their opposite numbers in the state corporations benefited similarly. Only the top jobs changed hands and their replacements were usually found from within the civil service. The conspicuous expenditure of the old CPP masters was cut out, but at the lower levels little changed and petty bribery and corruption remained endemic. The knowledge of this combined with the eventual resignation of General Ankrah in 1969 over the acceptance of funds from a group of businessmen diminished the credibility of the NLC. On the other hand, the relief felt within the civil service at the change of government eliminated the risk of sabotage or non-cooperation and even ensured a degree of constructive enthusiasm.

The smallness of the NLC and its members' lack of appreciation of the complexity of government led them to expect too much of delegation to officials. The notion of policy decisions, for example on the price of cocoa, as being the product of choice between imperfect alternatives and of compromise between a number of conflicting interests did not come naturally. The responsibility for decisionmaking quickly shifted in many cases to the more experienced officials, for even more than other governments newly in power the military in the NLC lacked the necessary expertise. At the same time the chastening experience of the previous ten years had made senior civil servants chary of questioning the proposals of their new masters when they made them: many of Nkrumah's prestige projects, such as the conference building in Accra, Job 600, and the international airline, would never have begun if civil servants had been allowed to advise on their practical financial feasibility. The military leadership quickly developed an irritable impatience with the inefficiencies and unpunctuality of civil servants at the lower levels. A part cause of some disillusionment at the higher levels was the remarkable determination of the Ghana civil service to maintain its political neutrality to which its essential survival from 1957 through to the 1970s must be regarded as a tribute.

In spite of difficulties, there were, however, broad areas of agreement that priority should be given to the problem of foreign debts and to rural developments, while prestige construction projects should be halted or run down. The NLC members for the most part did not, as their ministerial predecessors had done, become directly involved in problems of village water supply or the allocation of market stalls; a proper division of function between the political leadership and the administration began to appear. Gradually a working arrangement between the NLC members and civil servants emerged: this was a matter of particular concern to General Afrifa when he eventually succeeded General Ankrah. Indeed by 1968 such evidence as is available suggests a growth of mutual respect: for instance, General Ocran writes, 'The civil servants of Ghana have given us their fullest cooperation and made our work much easier. Only a few have dragged their feet. . . .'* Civil servants in their turn showed no enthusiasm for a return to civilian rule which would lead to unpredictable, and perhaps ill-educated, politicians breathing down their necks. These attitudes reflect the essential unity of the Ghana élite which enabled the inexperienced 'politicians' who constituted the NLC leadership to leave to their civilian counterparts the more general problems relating to trade and the economy while they concentrated on the maintenance of domestic authority and plans for a successor régime. In the event the army returned to barracks before intra-hierarchical dissension or any widespread discontent could emerge: to the extent that the NLC failed to live up to the expectations created the brunt seems to have been borne by its successor.

* *Ibid.*, 94.

As we have seen, the effect of the reforming régime on corruption was limited: by its alliances and its need to consolidate popularity it inhibited its 'cleansing' power. General Ankrah, after the Nigerian regional models of Colonels Ojukwu and Ejoor, tried to enforce harder work and punctuality on civil servants adjusted to a more leisurely tempo. The same factors affected the realization of a measure of austerity. Defence expenditure increased by 41 per cent between 1966 and 1969, and what is more it absorbed a greater proportion of foreign currency than any other departmental budget. It was arguable that Nkrumah's preference for the POGR and the sad state even of uniforms and boots at the time of the coup made this inevitable, but at the same time other groups – notably university lecturers and senior civil servants, especially lawyers and medical officers – were awarded increases of up to 40 per cent as a result of a Commission on the Structure and Remuneration of the Public Services which reported in 1968. This was at a time when expenditure on industrial and agricultural development, trade and communications, were being cut back by percentages as high as seventy. Again the justification that this reflects Nkrumah's extravagance in these directions may be partially sustained, but the charge that the application of austerity policies was selective is also capable of being upheld and has tended to reinforce the view that the standards acquired by African officers at e.g. Sandhurst have proved inappropriate in the socio-economic context of their own less developed countries. On the simplest level this might mean the adoption of the types of equipment appropriate to European armed forces and corresponding standards of living for the officer corps. There is, however, little evidence in Ghana of the first of these two categories of expenditure: reasonably sophisticated communications systems and air transport such as helicopters in limited numbers can be justified on grounds of efficiency. Moreover, action radically to reform pay and conditions could not have applied unilaterally to the armed forces.

The Ghana wages and salaries structure suffers in the same way as many other parts of Africa from the legacy of recent colonial rule and from the influence of international standards in certain fields, but it is not easy to reconcile any attempt at austerity and economy with the substantial increase in registrations of luxury private cars, such as Mercedes, which was apparent after the coup.

A more serious criticism of military rule 1966-9 may lie in the apparent predisposition of the NLC to rely heavily on foreign managerial skills and thereby to perpetuate economic dependence. The latent discontent of the initially enthusiastic anti-Nkrumah intelligentsia may be attributed to this. It came to a head over the handling of the large number of state enterprises bequeathed by Nkrumah, many of which were running at a loss. The introduction of foreign enterprise to finance re-development of these areas of activity was not popular, even though on the face of it inevitable, and became critical in the case of the Abbott Laboratories of the United States and the state pharmaceutical corporation. In this case the government appeared to have traded a major interest to the American company on markedly unfavourable terms and, what is more, subsequently dismissed the editors of two state-owned newspapers for criticizing the agreement and suggesting that those advising the NLC did not have the economic interests of the country at heart.

The handling of foreign debts, especially short-term supplier credits negotiated in dubious circumstances by the Nkrumah government, incurred similar criticism. Instead of repudiating a proportion of the debts as an avowedly nationalist administration would probably have done, the NLC aimed at rescheduling, and did not, it was felt, exploit the advantages of their favoured political position with the Western governments concerned. The approach was that of 'officers and gentlemen' and was held by their critics to be inappropriate to the desperate economic situation with which the country was faced.

On the other hand the systematic and careful preparations for the transfer to civilian rule were a model which will be rarely emulated. The Constitutional Commission which was set up to make preparations was clearly strongly influenced by British and American modes of thinking about the problem of the restraint of power. The determination to divide and separate the constitutional powers was such that the restraints on the executive might well result in a decision-making procedure too laborious and long-drawn-out for the needs of a developing country. In many respects the eventual transfer of power back to civilian rule amounted to a reversion to the known values of the colonial period. This is not intended in any pejorative sense, for it resulted in the first place in an election conducted more fairly than any in tropical Africa since independence. It did, however, indicate that in temporarily ruling by decree like a colonial administration before self-government the officers of the NLC had done little more politically than provide a breathing-space – an opportunity for reappraisal. The problems facing Dr Busia's administration, apart from the resolution of economic difficulties, were to find means of encouraging the controlled evolution of a lasting and stable political system, while – despite the protestations of General Afrifa – keeping a watchful eye on the military who could, by definition and history, no longer be entirely disinterested.

In the event there was a repetition in a number of ways of the circumstances which led to Nkrumah's overthrow in 1966 – economic difficulties, austerity budgets, political misjudgment, alienation of substantial sections of the population and resentment in the armed forces. Dr Busia's Progress Party had been more successful in terms of popular votes at the election of October 1969 than the CPP had ever been. But the impact on the farmers of the dramatic fall in world cocoa prices in 1971 was mishandled; international indebtedness rose and rescheduling of old liabilities was only a palliative. The 1971 budget prohibited imports of cars and television sets and the currency, a fortnight before Colonel Acheampong's coup, was devalued by 48·3 per cent. The restrictions revived all the manifestations of petty corruption and, apart from the constitutional abuses, the conditions of January–February 1966 were faithfully reproduced. Dr Busia never captured the imagination of the electorate who had voted him to power. Now he was opposed by the cocoa farmers from his own region, and by trades unionists who objected to the abolition of the TUC and draconian measures against striking workers.

The 1971 budget cut defence expenditure by 10 per cent. The reaction was immediate, and the charge made by the coup leader, Colonel Ignatius Acheampong, against the Prime Minister was almost exactly that made by Ocran against Nkrumah. He alleged that the government had started taking away from the armed forces even those few amenities and facilities enjoyed under the Nkrumah régime.

Objectively there was some justice in the view that the armed forces had not fared particularly well at the hands of Dr Busia. By one means or another half of those who had been in the rank of lieutenant-colonel or above in 1966 had been removed, though most were given reasonably prestigious civilian jobs. Moreover, their passing cleared the decks for the rapid promotion of majors to colonel and brigadier, though in its turn their good fortune created a renewed promotion block for others lower down the line. There was thus relative inexperience at the top combined with a potentially frustrated middle order. At the same time entry to officer rank was greatly restricted by reducing the cadet intake and effectively extending the training course. Inevitably there was controversy within the Busia government over the validity of a substantial defence budget and a cut-back in military expenditure for 1971–2 seemed inevitable. In spite of effectively immobilizing the air force and the navy by causing their aircraft and ships to lie idle through lack of maintenance and fuel, the army establishment could only just be sustained and allowed as it were to 'tick over'. Major exercises involving the expenditure of ammunition and the use of transport were impossible and pressures built up for the socially productive use of the armed forces. An outbreak of cholera and the need for flood relief provided natural outlets for their energies, but the army command was on the whole resistant to an extension of the rôle to, for example, co-operation with the police in the fight against crime.

By mid-1971, however, the forces were committed to deployment on development programmes of one kind or another. A general feeling of uncertainty about relations with the civil power and about their real rôle began to grow. The sudden retirement of Lieutenant-General M. Otu after three years as Chief of Defence Staff, followed by the early resignation of Brigadier J. R. K. Acquah from the appointment of Acting Army Commander to take up a job in the building industry, not only proved unsettling but left the whole army command in the hands of new young men. Colonel Acheampong was at this stage 1st Infantry Brigade Commander at Accra. In these circumstances the sharp decline in the real incomes of officers had maximum impact. Not only did the July 1971 budget exact a one per cent contribution to development from all workers with incomes in the officers' salary bracket, but their treasured vehicle allowance was abolished. This was partially restored after a few months, but the devaluation of December 1971 completed a process which brought about a drastic reduction in the standard of living of the Ghanaian élite, especially the military. Dr Busia's government had effectively created the condition for an 'officers' amenities' coup even if that was not exactly what it turned out to be.

Military grievances precipitated intervention, but this time the underlying economic malaise was more important and the new National Redemption Council recognized the need to rally the population behind more popular policies. The customary action was taken against the members of the Busia government and their assets, and eventually even General Afrifa, when he ventured out of retirement in his native village to Accra, with the apparent intention of intervention, was detained. But the austerity measures were cancelled and the currency revalued. The objective was clearly to be consensus based on economic progress and on popular measures in restraint of foreign exploitation.

The second military government of Ghana began by cancelling contracts with four British companies connected with construction projects under the Nkrumah régime, whose arrangements for the provision of credit to finance their own operations in the country were thought to be particularly disadvantageous. Civil servants' car allowances were restored, the rents for their official quarters cut and the development levy imposed in the last Busia budget abolished. These measures not only satisfied the critical elements in the élite for the time being, but aroused popular fervour such as was characteristic of the early days of Nkrumah's leadership. Colonel Acheampong then declared his intention of producing a 'Revolutionary Charter' which would lay down political principles for development, and diversified diplomatic relations, including a renewal of contact with Peking. An attempt to set up an advisory committee consisting partly of Ghanaians involved in foreign business enterprises, A. L. Adu and Daniel Chapman Nyaho in particular, incurred such criticism that it was dissolved after only forty-eight hours' existence. This reflected the strength of nationalist feeling and the general style of NRC policy.

The criteria adopted were in no sense ideological but entirely governed by an assessment of the national interest. For instance, the practice of marketing all except a limited quantity of cocoa via the London market was resumed at an early stage. A mixed economy had obvious advantages and there was prompt recognition of the need to expand exports, especially timber: to this end banks were encouraged to develop local investment loan procedures. Between January and April 1972 alone a substantial trade surplus was built up at the expense partly of increasing reliance on local food supply. Government-financed institutions, such as universities, were instructed to apply drastic economies and to run student residences in a style appropriate to the needs of the country. At each stage potentially unpopular consequences, such as large increases in food prices, were offset by measures calculated to foster nationalist fervour: the proposals for state participation in, for example, CAST (Consolidated African Selection Trust), Ashanti Goldfields, African Timber and Plywood, and the British Aluminium Company's mines were particularly popular, especially in light of the former military government's sanctioning of a new fifty-year lease for Lonrho on the goldfields. These steps, reactions to the attempted coup reported in July 1972 and to the death of Kwame Nkrumah in Bucharest, enabled the NRC to contemplate broadening its popular political base by harnessing former CPP elements at the grass-roots level.

Internationally, the obvious positive neutrality of the new government helped to overcome the qualms of the British and other Western governments about the displacement of Busia. State participation in major extractive industry was no surprise and the determined effort to straighten out the economy by self-help measures tended to produce a new climate for the discussion of the debts question. By the end of 1972 Ghana was suffering from a shortage of export credit in Europe but her trade figures for August indicated a 40 per cent increase in exports and a 14 per cent fall in imports. This was not only the result of an advantageous rise in world cocoa prices, but of a considerable increase in the sales of timber, gold and diamonds. For the first time for ten years or more the Ghanaian economy was beginning to justify the optimism felt at independence in 1957, though in fact the underlying problems probably remain. A favourable trade balance in 1972 was produced largely by direct controls on imports and, as already described, a dramatic increase in exports, but import restrictions may well only have proved acceptable at the time because of the large stocks built up during the Busia period. The likelihood of increasing shortages of rice, sardines – always an irritant fact in the Ghanaian economy – and raw materials remained. Subsidies on a number of essential items encouraged smuggling and a prices and incomes policy created the conditions for growing tension between Colonel Acheampong's NRC and the trades unions. On the other hand, the campaign for food-growing self-sufficiency produced a useful response and was undoubtedly facilitated by devolution of responsibility to the regions. Nevertheless in the economic field Colonel Acheampong needed sustained good fortune in the shape of a continuing high world price for cocoa and the discovery of fresh mineral deposits to be sure of avoiding the crises experienced by his predecessors.

Politically, the ease with which Ghana's second military régime survived its first year and more of office suggested the discovery of some new formula. It seemed not only to have taken a leaf out of its predecessor's book but to have learnt the necessary lessons. The circumstances of the two interventions in politics were comparable and their reactions similarly pragmatic. The difference lay in the new administration's overt demonstration of its concern for the national interest over a broad front, its ability apparently to disregard any external cultural affiliations and its willingness to run risks in order to satisfy the needs of a broad spectrum of supporters.

Steps to restrict foreign enterprise were calculated to avoid serious alienation while sustaining nationalist fervour. The steering of a more obviously middle path between the left-wing policies of Nkrumah and the conservative liberalism of the Busia mould of established élite seemed both deliberate and advantageous. In order to distinguish himself from Busia, Acheampong had at least to appear to swing the country back to a pan-Africanist line not unlike that of Nkrumah. The partial rehabilitation of Nkrumah's posthumous reputation was a logical development, but significantly, if paradoxically, was matched by the re-establishment of 24 February as a public holiday in celebration of the anniversary of the 1966 coup which overthrew him. Such a course of events did, however, facilitate the re-establishment in Ghanaian society of such well-known supporters of Nkrumah as Kojo Botsio and Kwesi Amoaka-Atta, a former Governor of the Bank of Ghana, who was employed by the NRC administration as an economic adviser. Acheampong was also shrewd enough to allow the press, especially the *Daily Graphic*, to express fairly militant left-wing views, while he consolidated his position with the students and other potentially militant groups by denouncing Busia's suggestion of dialogue with South Africa which had never been a viable stance in the Ghanaian context and was to all intents and purposes meaningless.

The NRC itself might be said optimistically to have provided final proof that tribal divisions are not a serious factor in Ghana politics. Colonel Acheampong, an Ashanti, worked closely from the first with the original engineers of the coup – Majors Agbo, Selomey and Baah, who were from different ethnic groups – and within the Council itself Ewes were well represented as they had been under Ankrah. Thus while ironically, in view of Dr Busia's own tribal affiliation, the elected civilian government had tended to be Akan in character, the new military régime was in large measure ethnically neutral. This was partly because under Busia a new political system had begun to emerge in which class interest groups were beginning to take over as the foci of loyalty from tribal and personal groupings. He had cultivated the cocoa farmers while antagonizing the city workers, and undermined the position of the two vital privileged groups, the civil service and the army, by eroding their amenities. By interfering with the judiciary and failing to insist that his ministers declared their assets as provided in the constitution, he failed to live up to the expectations on the basis of which he had been elected and prepared the way for the ready acceptance of the military.

The NRC naturally redressed the damage done to the army's and the civil service's loyalty by the withdrawal of privileges. The establishment of legitimacy seemed simpler than the circumstances in which power was again seized by the armed forces merited. Throughout their early months in office Ghana's military rulers managed to preserve the appropriate image as honest patriots. It seemed possible by mid-1973 that the NRC had an unusual achievement to its credit – namely, the gradual development of a changing attitude towards work on the part of the ordinary citizen and with it a realization that public and private standards were related, that personal financial advantage and denunciation of corrupt public servants was inconsistent. With this went a willingness and ability to treat liberally all but a tiny minority of Busia's supporters. At the same time generous treatment of the army was coupled with a serious attempt to control abuses and arrogant military behaviour, including occasional and little publicized attempts to interfere with the course of justice when members of the armed services were involved. Unlike the earlier military government, and in spite of relative inexperience in the middle ranks, the NRC has injected military personnel into the state corporation and lower levels of government on a rotating basis.

Though lacking any obvious doctrinal commitment Colonel Acheampong's régime demonstrated from the first a shrewd appreciation of the military's inherent political advantages and an understanding of the popular expectations on which survival depended. What he perhaps failed to appreciate was that, in spite of what has been said above, the administration was unusually isolated from the main civilian interest groups and lacked the means of effective consultation. This was both a weakness and a strength in that there were no debts to be paid and nothing in pawn. The thoroughgoing military nature of the régime was in some senses its basis but it suffered from the evident disadvantage that there were no important civilians who could, when necessary, become scapegoats for error and failure. With more vociferous press criticism the importance of the involvement of prestigious figures, perhaps from the old bourgeois establishment, was more likely to be appreciated.

Nevertheless, as the year 1973 proceeded a planned return to civilian rule in any form seemed a remote possibility and the long-term evolution of a mixed administration the most likely prospect. The plan to introduce a form of national service for graduates was itself a sign of a firm determination to increase the general sense of participation in the development of a community in the widest sense. Moreover, by August 1973 the cocoa boom, with the London 'spot' price reaching £945 per ton, began to give the Acheampong government some economic freedom of movement and enabled a substantial increase in wages primarily to assist the lowest income group in the public sector. A rise in gold and currency reserves and a record trade surplus in the earlier part of the year which facilitated a limited loosening of import controls, was accompanied by a warning from Colonel Acheampong that such improvements carried with them a heavy responsibility for reinvestment in the country. It seems as though a dramatic change in the terms of trade might give Ghana a unique opportunity to practice the principles of economic self-reliance.

In the following two years, however, following the inflation of oil prices after the Yom Kippur war the situation again deteriorated. Agricultural development especially in Ghana's Northern region compensated to some extent for the external pressures and this constituted the military government's most important practical achievement.

IV · Francophone Africa – Dahomey

Dahomey, in its twelve and a half years of independence, has acquired a certain notoriety in Africa as the country which has had more coups and more changes of government, in its short life as a nation state, than any other on the continent. A rough calculation shows at least six coups, six constitutions and eleven governments since 1960, not to mention a number of interregna, abortive coups and plots, strikes, scandals, abortive elections and a near civil war. The country has lived constantly on the political margin, and in the budgetary red, with a top-heavy Civil Service and a demoralized peasantry, a classic instance of unviability and instability.

These were the words of a correspondent writing in *West Africa**
on 12 February 1973 about the significance of Major Kerekou's government, which had then been in power less than four months. In an appraisal of the activities of the military in Africa in 1972 the same journal's leading article said,† 'a coup in Dahomey no longer interests anybody but the coup which ended civilian rule in Ghana was politically the most significant West Africa has known'. The return to power of the army in Dahomey was, even if only out of habit, always on the cards in the face of the sharp decline in morale and the growth of indiscipline which followed the restoration of the 'old guard' politicians on a rotating basis. The apparently successful and peaceful transfer of power from President Maga to President Justin Ahomadegbé on 7 May 1972 had in its own way com-

* No. 2906, 195.
† *West Africa*, No. 2898 of 25 December 1972.

pounded the sense of failure which resulted from the army's inability to make anything of military rule. The interest of Dahomey's case lies in the reasons for this almost total disappointment in the army as a régime and the corresponding possibility that Kerekou's coup and the subsequent appearance of a leftward swing may have marked a turning point. On the face of it the nomenclature 'revolution', a much abused term in the context of recent Dahomeyan political history, was even in this case something of an exaggeration, and armed forces so divided and unsettled by continuous involvement in politics were unlikely to make it a reality, except perhaps in crude nationalist, anti-colonialist terms.

The incentives to the military in Dahomey repeatedly to intervene in politics and the problems encountered by them in the process sprang from the same source. In the approach to independence and subsequently, the political system, if that it could be called, never adjusted satisfactorily to the tensions created by regional and ethnic interests. Political arrangements tended to be bilateral rather than multilateral, always leaving at least one vital interest isolated and unrepresented and therefore open to approaches by one of the participants in an existing uneasy coalition.

Apithy, Maga and Ahomadegbé emerged in succession as the leaders of sectional interests in Dahomey. They represented respectively the urban *évolué* Catholic south, the north and the Fon people. The requirements of elections for the French National Assembly before 1959 and the interventions of Houphouet-Boigny from the Ivory Coast to 'settle' political crises in fact helped to produce at independence a ridiculously uneasy and shifting situation. At one time Maga and Apithy, who was a member of his government, were negotiating independently and separately making trade agreements with Western and Eastern European nations at the same time. Maga's appointment of Apithy as ambassador to France and his private negotiations with Ahomadegbé in opposition precipitated a crisis which Apithy effectively turned into a national versus regional power dispute. A succession of incidents centred round, in particular, a deputy in the National Assembly, Christophe Bohiki, who was alleged to have been implicated in the murder of an Apithy supporter, led to demonstrations in Porto Novo and a demand for military intervention. The trades union authority (*Union Générale des Travailleurs du Dahomey*) called a general strike and backed action by Colonel Christophe Soglo, Chief of Staff of the armed forces. President Maga's government was overthrown and for a two-month interregnum Dahomey experienced its first period of military rule with the army acting as it were on behalf of the trades unions. Maga having been removed because of an alleged northern assassination plot, there ensued a two-year coalition between Ahomadegbé and Apithy with Soglo and the army in the background.

This first episode effectively established the pattern of Dahomey's recurrent crises over ten years. The rivalry between personalities who, like repertory actors, shifted from rôle to rôle, was the characteristic feature: in the event the coup of December 1969 was about the same personal rivalries as the intervention in 1963. To change the metaphor, all the army had done in the first place was to act as a referee sending the players off to the touchline for two months while virtually nothing happened in midfield and then restarting the match after the interval and little real disciplinary action. Refurbished political institutions provided no adequate basis for a fresh start. The new party, Parti Démocratique Dahoméen (PDD), as before embraced only two out of the three main interest groups. Apithy, though nominally President, was second string to Ahomadegbé because of the latter's effective manipulation of the assembly and the party. The situation was almost a replica of what it had so disastrously been in 1959–60. One stood for Pan-Africanism, East European and Communist Chinese cooperation, the other for the French-speaking entente and collaboration with Western Europe and Taiwan. A clash over the presidency of the Supreme Court led to Ahomadegbé, as Vice-President and Premier, overthrowing Apithy with the aid of youth organizations and young officers.

At this point trades union discontent once more publicly manifested itself. The government was, not unreasonably, charged with failing to recognize the interests of organized labour not only by failing to pay workers adequately, but by not living up to their own austerity programme and devoting themselves to personal rivalries instead of to a national development plan. Disorder followed in which the soldiers refused to fire on the demonstrating crowd and General Soglo arrived to countermand the orders of the Prime Minister. The questioning of orders by the rank and file in this way may conceivably have been connected with an incident some years before when a Professor Adotévi had been invited to lecture to the troops and had concentrated on revolutionary theory and the duties of governments, which were now clearly not being carried out. The day after the rioting the army dismissed Ahomadegbé and Apithy and appointed a northerner, Tahirou Congacou, as head of a provisional government, but within a month General Soglo was Head of State. The Soglo régime lasted from December 1965 to December 1967: its decline and ultimate demise was due to failure on a number of fronts and not exclusively to its failure to make any headway in resolving the country's virtually insoluble economic problems. The labour unions, the complications involved in managing a governmental machine and above all intergenerational rivalries within the army were responsible.

There was no doubting the seriousness of the economic problem to which the deep malaise which has continually affected the southern part of Dahomey is largely attributable. President Soglo recognized the prime priority of economic recovery and the need for an adequate local effort if the flow of French help was to continue. Members of the government made ritual appearances working on local agricultural and road construction

programmes. But the Soglo government's appeal for retrenchment and a return to the land held little attraction for south-
erners induced away from agricultural projects in search of
white-collar employment in the towns, particularly Cotonou
and Porto Novo. An austerity programme which included a 25
per cent wage cut by direct taxation caused a direct confrontation with the unions and eventually led to intervention on the
part of young officers to prevent a general strike.

Officially the government made plans for the increase of
agricultural production and diversification. A five-year development plan initiated in 1966 allotted one-third of the total
funds available to rural development and slightly less to the
development of local processing industries which would help to
make substantial savings on the importation of processed
goods. The development plan assumed, however, that nearly
90 per cent of the investment funds required would have to
come from external sources and special steps were taken to
convince the French that this would be worthwhile. To this end
General Soglo's special relationship with General de Gaulle was
vital. Austerity involving a range of cuts and taxes beyond that
already mentioned brought conflict with the unions. Though
some limited progress was made the trade deficit increased and
was greater than at any time since independence in 1966 when
exports covered the cost of less than one-third of the total imports.

These were circumstances in which the lack of confidence of
the unions in government was almost inevitable but there is
little doubt that the situation was made worse by the deterioration in relationships between the Soglo government and the
unions. While the unions shrewdly realized that the military
needed them as a power base, the military step-by-step took
power into their own hands and in fact withdrew existing
opportunities for union participation in the decision-making
process. Nor was it only the unions which considered members
of the government as high-handed technicians – an attitude

reinforced by the abolition of the National Renovation Committee after a few months of power. The French business community resented their somewhat crude treatment, as did civil servants. On one occasion a customs official was reportedly imprisoned for trying to charge army officers duty on whisky brought across the frontier.

At this point the military in office were making the fundamental errors characteristic of brash and unsophisticated military régimes: they failed conspicuously to live up to their own precepts, neglected properly to cultivate interest groups vital to the credibility of their authority, and they gave the impression of subordinating national interests to the political expedients necessary to secure foreign aid. Success in tackling economic problems might have altered the situation but this was scarcely feasible.

The sequence of events in the Dahomeyan crisis of December 1967 not only displayed the full range of characteristics which tend to consolidate the establishment of army rule, but revealed the essential problems of military régimes in French-speaking Africa. On 8 December 1967 the union of primary school teachers declared a forty-eight hour strike in support of salary claims. The Soglo government's predictable response was to declare all trades union activity suspended on the grounds of misuse of trades union rights. This action originated with the Military Vigilance Committee (set up early in 1967 by younger officers primarily to curb the power of General Soglo) and amounted to a declaration that the strike was illegal. In the event the school teachers defied the ban and were supported by other workers seeking to obtain the withdrawal of the 25 per cent tax on salaries which in various forms had operated since June 1965. The government claimed that this resistance to essential government austerity measures was a step towards anarchy brought about by professional agitators and undermined their attempt to obtain more aid from France on the basis of the continuation of a stern policy of retrenchment. The

strike spread to post and telecommunications workers but the
government, though it ordered the arrest of sixteen trades
union leaders, still made some attempt to avoid a final show-
down with the unions. By 12 December progress seemed to have
been made towards some limited agreement and an attempt
was made to call off the threatened general strike and to invite
the strikers already out to return to work. The following day,
however, the strike spread to the railways and airports were
closed. At this stage Colonel Alley, the army commander, took
the initiative in speaking to union leaders and saying that he
would act as the unions' spokesman before the Council of
Ministers the following day. The Council met and refused
to release the arrested union leaders. Two hundred troops
were drafted to Cotonou and Porto Novo. But the strike continued.

At this point there appears to have been a division between
senior army officers, possibly along tribal or regional lines.
Major Maurice Kouandeté from the north refused to attend a
meeting with Colonel Alley to protest against alleged appease-
ment of the unions. Alley had already resisted pressures to lead
an overthrow of the government. The following morning two
parachute commando units, with whose establishment Alley
had been closely associated, surrounded his house, and the
houses of President Soglo, of the Minister of the Interior, and of
the chairman of the Military Vigilance Committee. The young
officers set up a Military Revolutionary Committee to replace
their own, earlier Military Vigilance Committee, but the problems remained the same – a small, complacent, entrenched and
relatively well-educated urban middle class and a growing mass
of unemployed workers in the south contrasting with some improvement in living standards in the northern rural areas where
expectations were lower.

Led by Kouandeté and Kerekou, officers from the northern
Somba tribes, they claimed that the government had been
paralysed by corruption and the Vigilance Committee silenced.

The economic and social situation had deteriorated, and, most significantly, according to a radio broadcast 'the peasant masses, who were constantly asked to make a greater effort, were wearing themselves out with work without seeing their lot improved or changed'. The government were 'drunk with power' and had behaved 'like veritable potentates'. The same broadcast announced the establishment of a constitutional committee leading to a referendum, the free popular election of representatives and the establishment of 'democratic' institutions. The pledge to transfer power to popular political leaders at the moment of its seizure implied a considerable trust in the political commonsense of the Dahomeyan people which did not seem to correspond with the officers' disgust concerning union activities.

It is interesting to note that Dr Zinsou, who later became President, declined to serve in the provisional government. The government met at the army camp near Cotonou and denied its regional roots or any foreign or internal political affiliation. Colonel Alley, still apparently head of the army, openly expressed his doubts to journalists as to the need to seize power and spoke of the possibilities which had existed for reforming the old system. The following day, however, he was still under house arrest and General Soglo seems to have taken refuge in the French Embassy. The trades unions demanded a greater voice for organized labour and, in particular, the elimination of the political influence of France and America over the Dahomeyan Government. Protests against French 'neo-colonialism' have, for obvious reasons, not generally been upheld by Francophone military régimes.

At a meeting between the Revolutionary Committee and the trades unions the dilemma was clearly stated. The annulment of the 25 per cent cut in wages combined with a refusal of French aid would result in a budget deficit of nearly £4 m.: even the payment of civil servants for the current month was at stake because the money was not available in the treasury. The demands of the unions combined with the fragile financial position constituted a serious problem for the provisional administration. By 21 December the problem was of such severity that it was clear that the Revolutionary Committee lacked sufficiently broadly-based support to survive. Colonel Alley was therefore brought into the government as Head of State while retaining command of the army.

In a broadcast to the nation on 22 December Alley referred to the indivisibility of the army as being 'the only organised force in the country, where political parties have so far been mere electoral movements. Twice already, *at the request of the people*, the Dahomeyan army has been obliged to assume power.' He promised a return to constitutional government and elections 'within a maximum period of six months, no matter the circumstances'. Thus Alley emerged as leader to resolve the tensions which had developed within an army attempting to function politically in a situation of grave economic difficulty. It was not enough to demonstrate that the government and peasants were one, as Soglo's ministers had done by working beside them in the fields, nor to criticize a departure from that degree of commitment to austerity. The restlessness of the young educated élite within the army itself needed the restraint of mature leadership capable of mediation with militant civil groups. In particular, the traditional military mistrust of trades unions required modification if the Dahomey economic crisis were not to deteriorate into paralysis and permanent deadlock, resolvable only by a degree of force which had not recently been a feature of life in Cotonou or Porto Novo.

The dominance in the minds of Dahomeyan leaders of the economic problem led to a degree of urgency about the return to legality and to constitutional rule unparalleled elsewhere in Africa. Alley's acceptance of office towards the end of December 1967 was followed by announcement of a referendum on 31 March 1968 with a view to a return to civilian rule on 17 June. The referendum was to determine the validity of a constitution drawn up in February. The whole operation combined shrewd political appreciation with brisk military efficiency which many associated with the personal qualities of Colonel Alley.

Alley represents the younger generation of fully French-trained army officers in Africa: in other words he is strictly a professional and as such not particularly attracted to involvement in politics; like many of his contemporaries, he essentially despises politicians. He comes from Bassila near the border with Dahomey in what may be termed the north-central region of the country. His father, a soldier in the French army, was in charge of training the Togo police in the 1930s. Alley went at an early stage to the school for children of soldiers at Bingerville in the Ivory Coast and to a military secondary school in Dakar. He belongs strictly to the mobile West African élite, cosmopolitan in outlook, and served in Indo-China, Morocco and Algeria within a short time of first joining the French army. He became a paratrooper with all the associations which that rôle had in North Africa and subsequently established such a unit in Dahomey. He returned to independent Dahomey as a lieutenant.

Alley's first real introduction to political matters came with Soglo's in 1963. Riots in the main Dahomeyan towns forced the army to intervene and briefly to put affairs again on the right track. Reintervention by the army two years later in November 1965 appeared to Alley and others in the same professional cast as simply a means of preventing bloodshed by separating Apithy and Ahomadegbé, who seemed on the verge of leading their factions into collision with one another. A month later the inadequacy of such an approach was demonstrated when the army had to take over full power. Nevertheless the function of reconciliation between groups clearly had a high priority in the minds of the military leadership. The political parties must be brought together in a sense of national purpose in order to avoid a decline into regionalism. Alley was more like Afrifa in

Ghana and Gowon in Nigeria than like the father figures of the first generation of military leaders. An article in *West Africa** pointed out Alley's similarities to Gowon, such as that Alley, like Gowon, came from a small tribe between the north and the south, which made him, with his professional record, a natural champion of national unity. His training gave him an almost puritanical concern to cleanse corruption and an inclination to resist Soglo's view that the army, having seized power, should stay to see the development plan through.

It is not easy to assess to what extent Alley, having ended up in power himself, dissociated himself from the faults in Soglo's régime in order to proclaim his own political innocence. It is perhaps fairest to judge him by his actions in rapidly initiating the return to civilian rule at a speed unparalleled in Sierra Leone, where it ought to have been easier, or in Ghana. Certainly he was able to avoid excessive entanglement in the decline of Soglo's administration by being away for a period on a course in Paris and by being able to devote himself almost exclusively to military affairs. Corruption and a return to legality certainly ceased to be regarded as urgent issues within a year of Soglo's assumption of power. Typically, but perhaps with less than justice, the President was seen to have become just another politician. In the end his tactlessness in handling army discontent may have been decisive in causing his overthrow, for the motivation of the strikes appeared to be running out by the time the coup took place on 17 December 1967. This illustrated Soglo's political inexperience, and the outcome perhaps illustrated Alley's greater realism when faced with a nonmilitary situation. Kerekou and Kouandeté must at some point have realized the weakness of their own relatively inflexible position and taken account of the prestige value of Alley's authority and, indeed, the need to conciliate the French without whose very recent financial concessions to Soglo the task of reconstruction was bound to prove much greater. In fact the

* *West Africa*, No. 2652, 30 March 1968, 365.

essential budget aid from Paris was denied and Alley's programme was thus more difficult to implement.

Politically Alley tended from the first to see national unity in
single party terms. It is arguable that this is a natural standpoint for the military trained mind. It may be too that the
referendum of 31 March 1968 on the proposed constitution for
civilian rule gave Dahomey's leaders food for thought about
their own political potential, for 92 per cent of the votes cast
were in favour. In some areas, like Colonel Alley's home town,
Bassila, the figure was 100 per cent. This seemed to suggest a
Dahomeyan capacity for political organization, but a combination of the older politicians, whose capacity for survival
could only be rated as remarkable but who were probably so
imbued with the political mores of the French Fourth Republic
that a period of stable government would have come as a surprise to them, with a volatile military slow to learn its political
lessons, portended more political agonizing for Dahomey.

The young officers who wished understandably to ban Maga,
Apithy and Ahomadegbé from the presidential contest under
the new constitution were at one and the same time optimistically unrealistic and cynical. The elimination of the veterans
could only have been achieved satisfactorily by installing
credible civilian substitutes conjured up by a military leadership which had found the secret of reconciling military intervention with the revival of political life. Once having attempted
to 'cleanse' politics of its impurities officers have found great
difficulty in accepting again the – from their point of view –
imperfections of civilian rule. The subsequent imposition of
conditions for the return to full political life resembles the
struggle which colonial administrators once had in envisaging
the transfer of power to their successors. The fact is that military governments have tended to have standards of particular
kinds not obviously shared with the rest of the community: this
has often seemed to be the biggest obstacle to the transfer of
power back to civilian hands. An example of this may be taken

even from the first three months of Colonel Alley's period of office in Dahomey. In January 1968 a special Military Tribunal was set up to deal with cases of embezzlement of public funds and bribery. At the beginning of April its decisions were declared null and void and a new body called the Military Correction Committee was set up in its place to reconsider all the cases already heard as well as new ones. Major Kouandeté gave as the reason for this the unsatisfactory attitudes of some of the civilian magistrates on the original tribunal which, he said, amounted almost to obstruction. Contempt for the non-military and the consistent adoption of a 'holier than thou' outlook is perhaps the most serious general obstacle to demilitarization.

The farcical and in a way tragic interlude between the announcement of the presidential election to take place in April/May 1968 and the sudden, surprise installation of Dr Émile Zinsou as President in June is worth recording largely because it illustrated clearly, at any rate in the Dahomeyan situation, the recurrent inability of the army to achieve any radical break with the political past or to neutralize the traditional interests. The enmeshment of the army in the general political situation – involving as it did, in the competition between Alley and Kouandeté, a corresponding rivalry to that between the recognized politicians – was, of course, at the root of the problem.

In the event the trio of former Presidents were disqualified and the five candidates whose nominations were accepted by the Council of Ministers were of no great significance and only one of them had had any substantial political experience. The ensuing call by Maga and Apithy for a boycott fell on fertile ground in view of the known attitudes of the younger army officers, and it is worth noting that the Supreme Court's ruling that their disqualification was unconstitutional had been bypassed by the government. At the election only one candidate, Dr Basile Adjou Moumouni, secured a substantial number of votes. In the political domains of ex-Presidents Maga and

Apithy less than 3 per cent of the electorate voted and, according to Colonel Alley, the figure for the country at large was only 24 per cent. This result was more than an embarrassment to the military government: it amounted to a fundamental rejection of its political judgment. There seemed to be no alternative to a postponement of the return to civilian rule which had been promised for 17 June. Colonel Alley, however, repeated the interim government's intention of seeking a candidate who would attract a broad consensus of support.

In the meantime Maga and Apithy were once again manoeuvring in Paris with a view to a joint candidature for the presidency, to which they appeared to claim the abortive election had established their moral right. At the same time Ahomadegbé, also from Paris, had upheld the validity of Dr Adjou's election, alleging intimidation of his potential supporters in a number of parts of the country, though it was not clear how the other two ex-Presidents could have achieved the level of abstentions recorded in Cotonou. His announcement did not assist the resolution of the crisis because in spite of his less obtrusive interference and his comparatively modest life style it reinforced the belief that he, as much as Maga and Apithy, regarded power in Dahomey as a personal perquisite. Alley thus had no alternative but to continue his search for a popular candidate. He stressed in a speech to the nation, 'Our only objective is to achieve at any cost the return to legality.' He attempted to work through the representatives of the three banned political parties, and was faced with a union threat of a general strike if the army did not return to barracks on the appointed date, which seemed a sure recipe for national chaos.

It is against this background that the designation of Dr Zinsou as President for a nominal five-year term must be judged. He had been on the additional list of those excluded from candidacy for the presidential election in April 1968 and in no real sense represented a break with the old political 'order'. Foreign Minister in Maga's government until 1963, he had been recalled to Soglo's administration at the end of 1965. He seemed to appeal to the younger officers as representing in the least harmful way the need in the face of problems over French aid for a degree of continuity in international relations, but his power base within the country was weak. Though this manoeuvre bought time in the shape of an interval of seventeen months between changes of government, the omens were poor. In the first place, it caused a temporary rapprochement, in Paris, between ex-Presidents Maga, Apithy, Ahomadegbé and Soglo. The three civilians were outspokenly condemnatory of the rôle of the military, who they regarded as uneducated amateurs in politics. Their first reaction was to form with the unions the National Front for Democratic Struggle to combat the Zinsou régime.

Free from military interference Dr Zinsou's administration might have emerged as a creditable compromise; it did in fact attempt to tackle the overriding social and economic problems but though nominally in the background the army remained the decisive force. What Kouandeté, on seizing power, described as a reassumption of its responsibilities by the army had an air of inevitability about it: to claim, as he did, that it was a continuation of its rôle in maintaining peace and political stability must have seemed to many a statement undeserving of dispassionate evaluation. Dr Zinsou's dilemma clearly reflected the problem of successor civilian régimes once the military have had the taste of power. He had to choose between rivals within the military arm for his support and backed the personal ambitions of Kouandeté, an able French-trained officer of the new generation, who had come off second-best to Alley in the 1968 coup. Alley in his turn sought to eliminate Kouandeté in an attempted coup in July 1969 and was brought to trial. This led Zinsou to think in terms of the replacement of Kouandeté in a genuine search for a demilitarized régime. Gaston Fouru, the prosecutor at Alley's trial, was reported to have said, 'What we must stop is a situation where the gun is a means of promotion, a machine gun a way of applying pressure, a tank becomes government policy. . . . We must stop changes of régime every two years, otherwise Dahomey will soon go out of existence as a nation.'*

Be that as it may, Kouandeté's coup led to the immediate return to Dahomey of Maga, Apithy, Ahomadegbé and even Soglo. The ritual *pas de trois* of the politicians was soon resumed under a formalized arrangement for their rotation. In spite of Kouandeté's claim concerning the rôle of the army, nothing appeared to have been achieved. The frequent changes of government had aborted economic development, while the evolution of a stable political system seemed more remote than ever. The rotating three-man presidency had simply institu-tionalized instability and soon discarded any illusions of austerity. The army itself was the main threat to the new régime's continuity. The interaction of the personalities of Alley, Kouandeté and Kerekou had become as complex, con-fusing and repetitive as that of the three politicians. The character of civil–military relations in Dahomey could best be summed up in the career of Alphonse Alley. Instrumental in persuading General Soglo to overthrow the Maga régime in 1963 and the Ahomadegbé–Apithy administration in 1965, in 1970 he was promoted to serve as Secretary-General of Defence the three-man presidency of those he had previously worked to displace. At this point the credibility of the Dahomeyan army rested on its ability, as it were, 'to find its soul' and determine on a radical and united break with the past. The question two years later was whether this was the significance of Kerekou's intervention.

Throughout 1971 and the earlier part of 1972 various mani-festations of army unrest and disarray kept Dahomeyan poli-ticians on tenterhooks. Officers defied the authorities in releasing felons from jail – Kouandeté himself suffered a sentence of detention for just this – concealing the Togolese opposition

* *West Africa*, No. 2742, 20 December 1969, 1535.

leader Noë Kutuklui and refusing to testify at a trial arising from the mutiny of a paracommando unit at Ouidah. These conditions were ideal for the consolidation of Captain Mathieu Kerekou, a northerner from the same ethnic group as Kouandeté. The coup threatened in February 1972 following the mutiny became a reality on 26 October, with Kerekou the natural leader following the successive discrediting of Soglo, Alley and then Kouandeté. The release of officers imprisoned as a result of the mutiny and the appointment to ministerial positions of officers with clear political orientation were important steps in consolidating Kerekou's authority, especially as he assumed the army to be the font of political power and was not prepared to share it with civilians. The timing of the coup was, however, arbitrary: the law and order position had improved, the economy was not sharply deteriorating and a charge that educational reform had been badly organized by the Presidential Council seemed a somewhat esoteric excuse. Extravagance and corruption in high places was scarcely new, though a crisis over a stationery monopoly provided an appropriately operetta-style touch.

The full militarization of the administration involved for the first time the systematic retirement of all the more senior officers to the point where almost all those in key posts were of the same vintage and similarly educated. The significance of the virtual elimination of officers of the French army did not escape French observers. Veterans of Indo-China and Algeria were now scarce. The extent to which this was the result of left-wing ideological pressures on Kerekou was not, however, clear: the Dahomeyan left is very diverse and lacks cohesion. Kerekou himself appeared to be seeking popularity by exploiting quasi-Marxist opinion which had for long found expression in tracts circulating in Cotonou. The changed climate reflected itself in, for example, mass student demonstrations outside Western embassies against the assassination of Amilcar Cabral. Incidents at this time involving Frenchwomen worried the

French community. The resumption of relations with Peking raised the question of the main source of aid, for apart from the fact that China might benefit from a possible foothold in this part of West Africa, Dahomey was likely to be only a liability and occasionally an embarrassment to any power that befriended her.

It is, however, true to say that for the first time since independence Dahomey in 1972–3 acquired an administration consisting of young, energetic, like-minded men. The cries of 'self-reliance' and 'national independence' vaguely echoed the pronouncements of Colonel Acheampong's régime in Ghana. Kerekou's early statements referred to the legacy of intertribal conflicts, political oppression and economic exploitation, with the emphasis on the latter in the shape of foreign domination. His proposals for reform involved not only steps to absorb foreign commercial enterprises into the national pattern but a reform of educational and cultural provision so as firmly to weaken connections with France and also with organizations associated with the imperial period – OCAM (Organisation Commune Africaine et Malgache), Air Afrique and the West African Central Bank. The recognition of Peking may have been only symbolic. The question remained as to the extent to which the currency question could be tackled and French aid dispensed with.

Major Kerekou's problem remains in essence that of Colonel Acheampong in Ghana – how to reconcile national aspirations with the need for foreign investment and the satisfaction of domestic interest groups. It is, however, hard to believe that even after ten years of recurrent crisis Dahomey has finally, by the agency of an often fissile army, lived down its history of perverse personal and ethnic rivalries and its inclination to govern by intrigue and conspiracy.

To describe Dahomey as typical of Francophone Africa in these respects would clearly be an exaggeration. In Upper Volta, for example, the consequences of economic unviability and army attempts to tackle it lacked the extravagant fantasy of the neighbouring country, but then a semi-desert country with a small urban population distributed in towns which were little more than villages by other standards provided a different climate. Some might claim that French education and military training had, by creating the illusion of sophistication, surely endowed the Dahomeyan élite with a propensity for political games. What is in this connection noteworthy is the survival in 1973, alive and active in their way, of almost all the first performers on the Dahomeyan political scene – a monument perhaps to a cultural situation which encouraged an emphasis on personalities and ploys and for a long period minimized the development of a true professionalism in any field.

V · The Rôle of the Military in Nigeria 1966–74

Any discussion of the rôle of the Nigerian military after the beginning of 1966 must in the first place take into account the total transformation of the army in the subsequent three to four years. Effectively thinned by the coups of 1966, its original personnel suffered further heavy casualties serving on both sides in the civil war, while the residue was in any case massively diluted by the twentyfold expansion of the federal forces necessitated by that war. In the early hours of 15 January 1966 a small group of army officers, variously calculated in number as between fourteen and thirty (seven majors and twenty-three more junior officers), staged a military coup against a civilian government which was essentially that which had taken power at independence in October 1960. By their actions, especially in Lagos and Kaduna, they set in train a series of violent events the long-term outcome of which, in terms of the political development and stability of Nigeria, is not yet clear. The conspirators were themselves in most cases to rank amongst the major casualties of their own initiative: their personal success, if such it can be termed, was even by the standards of *coups d'état* exceptionally shortlived. In any real sense their unusually clearly defined political objectives have never been achieved: an unbroken period of military rule, punctuated in its early stages by counter-coup and civil war, has, however, ensued.

The coincidental emergence of Nigeria not only as the largest but also as the most important and influential country in Africa is sufficient to compel an appraisal of the performance of the military in government, first under Major-General J. T. U. Aguiyi Ironsi, then under the younger General Yakubu Gowon. The responsibility of Ironsi's government for the renewal of violence in mid-1966, the rôle of Gowon's government in the period leading up to the attempted secession of Biafra, its conduct of the war, handling of postwar reconstruction and reconciliation and finally its domestic and external performance all invite assessment and in a variety of ways throw light on the capacity of the military to conduct affairs not strictly of a professional character. But as part of an historically continuous process the army during the early part of this period first largely disintegrated and was then reconstituted: an appreciation of the physiological changes in the military body is, therefore, fundamental to an understanding of the Nigerian case.

During the first coup in January 1966 a small number of officers killed the premiers of the Western and Northern regions as well as the internationally distinguished federal Prime Minister, Sir Abubakar Tafawa Balewa. They also eliminated a number of senior army officers who, in their judgment, would be likely to obstruct their plans. With two exceptions, one political, one military, all those assassinated were Northerners or Westerners: Yakubu Gowon and Hassan Katsina, moreover, were the most notable officers to avoid death on this occasion. Correspondingly, of those who took an active part in the coup at least five-sixths were from the East and Mid-West regions, the majority of them Ibos. Though it is demonstrable that their objectives were national and ideological rather than regional and factional, the conspirators soon came to be seen as having organized an Ibo coup against the other ethnic groups. Whatever the reality it was this apparent truth which was to dominate the events immediately to come. For Ironsi, the officer commanding the small original force of about 10,000 men, who intervened and without difficulty persuaded the demoralized politicians to hand over power without further violence, the legend of the Ibo coup or conspiracy was quickly to prove disastrous. What might, in other circumstances, have seemed not wholly unreasonable steps towards the achievement of national unity simply added to the existing anger and suspicion. The coup of 15 January was seen as depriving the North of power, and with each of Ironsi's moves the shift seemed to be confirmed. A civilian uprising in the North in May was followed by the assassination of Ironsi and many other Easterners in the army at the end of July. At this point Lieutenant-Colonel Odumegwu Ojukwu, the military governor of the Eastern region, managed to consolidate the Ibos in their heartland and around the regional capital, Enugu. Not only the nation but also the army was now effectively divided into hostile parts and the attempted secession of Biafra at the end of May 1967 was on the cards.

The initial coup had politically radical purposes: it sought to overthrow a conservative Northern-dominated régime in the interests of a new concept of 'one Nigeria'. In so doing it accentuated the cleavages which already existed within the army itself. These were the product of a mélange of factors affecting the pattern of recruitment over the previous two decades. The requirements of British imperial policy with its insistence on politically neutral soldiers with a martial tradition from remote areas had been initially the most important of these, especially when by contrast the majority of officers were recruited from near the urban areas in the South where the best educational opportunities existed. The resulting predominance of Northern and Middle Belt other ranks, and conversely of Ibo and other Eastern officers in the middle of the army hierarchy constituted a dangerous incongruence in a situation in which political control of the defence forces was in Northern hands. While expatriate British officers remained in key positions the cleavages were masked and the chances of a major challenge to hierarchical authority by subordinates remained slight.

When the crisis came the cause was not a relatively simple intergenerational rivalry: indigenous authority had not had the time or the conditions in which to become consolidated to the point where subordinates naturally accepted its legitimacy and behaved accordingly. The behaviour of the rebels was, however, in itself ambivalent: having apparently rejected authority, as professionals they continued to respect the conventions of military status. This may account for Major Nzeogwu's curious submission, at long distance, to the authority of Major-General Ironsi; it certainly contributes to an understanding of men who combined strongly Pan-African sentiments and anti-white racial attitudes with the country gentleman and 'man-about-town' postures of British officers. This leads on to the view that while the Nigerian coups were certainly about the distribution of power in society they were also to a degree spontaneous, emotional, and in the event not wholly successful, protests against an institutional structure in which the people concerned knew themselves to be enmeshed and part of the norms of which they at least subconsciously accepted.

The volatile political conditions prevailing in many developing countries reveal the weaknesses and concealed paradoxes of the military situation. Where there is uncertainty about the duty owed to a political authority whose legitimacy is in question for any reason, then the inherent conflict between discipline and a high level of independent initiative, which is an essential feature of military institutions, is heightened. The appearance, even illusion, of the military as a rigid bureaucracy is sustained in developed countries with long traditions because the tests to which it is subjected are normally strictly military. If it was as rigid as it seems, and as the civilian conventionally supposes, then it would collapse when subjected to operational strains. Effective and rapid response to crises requires flexibility and discretion of a high order. This is in fact achieved within armed forces not by rules and regulations, but by the establishment of a graduated range of responsibilities and duties, the successful carrying out of which depends on the personality or charismatic qualities of the officer at each level. The functioning of an army depends on the flexibility of the response of subordinates to the orders of their supervisors and on the successful transmission of orders down a chain of command involving a large measure of discretion: the capacity to delegate responsibility for decisions and not to interfere with them once taken is an important characteristic of the successful military commander.

All these qualities were inadequately developed in the Nigerian army as it stood at the beginning of 1966. In a situation of political unrest and severe inter-group tension imbalances and dysfunctional features emerged. On the one hand, the rules were used to justify the carrying out of unprofessional orders, while at the same time there was on occasion a supreme disregard for the deference due to status as in the systematic assassination of senior officers in January 1966. Indeed it could be argued that the events of the night 14/15 January 1966 were the product not of an ethnic conspiracy but of a consistent attempt to eliminate the whole command structure of the army. The fact that those killed were primarily of Northern and Western regional origin may simply have reflected the existing position within the hierarchy and the good fortune of those from other parts of the country who survived. The Nigerian military structure seems to have lacked at the time the full apparatus of controls and safety valves which normally enables military institutions to survive disruptive tensions. One factor in delaying its development may well have been the combination of a politically deteriorating situation, especially in the Western region, with a rapid rate of localization of the officer corps.

The problems of Africanization have usually been seen in terms of the quantity of young officers commissioned and the corresponding speed of their replacement of expatriates. In the last resort, however, the extent of the experience and training of senior officers may have proved to be just as important. The Nigerian forces in 1966 included just twenty-two officers with

staff training at the Camberley Staff College, the Pakistan
Staff College, Quetta, the US Command and Staff College at
Fort Leavenworth, or their equivalents. At this level the
degree of what may be termed military socialization was slight.
On the other hand, it is well known that the Nigerian army of
1966 was an inherited force: it consisted of units of the Royal
West African Frontier Force recruited in Nigeria or in a few
cases from adjoining territories. It was not a new organization
but it required adapting to the needs of an independent African
state and in particular it needed to identify its rôle, which in
strategic terms had been imperial and for internal purposes was
essentially to act in aid of a colonial civil power.

Though at the time of the coup only relatively few officers
had completed conventional staff training, the career patterns,
based on progressive courses often outside Nigeria, were established. Nigerian officers had been by no means unsuccessful in
emulating their contemporaries while attending institutions not
only in the countries already mentioned, but in India, Ethiopia,
Canada and Australia. They had, surprisingly from the standpoint of 1960 and the predictions of some of the most intelligent
among them, including the then Captain Ojukwu, acquired the
social patina and adopted the institutions, notably the officers'
mess, of their mentors. The hierarchy, the institutions and the
relevant ritual had been handed on. It was, however, some of
the more important conventions which turned out to be fragile
to the point of non-existence in the kind of crisis which the
country faced.

The fragility of the professional conventions was, however, in
some senses due, not only to lack of experience and the absence
of a native tradition, but to a mismatch between their source
and the institution in which they were now supposed to apply.
The merits of hierarchy and of personal authority based on
status are less obvious in an organization where small differences in age and length of service separate the top from the
bottom. Career patterns and promotion prospects for Nigerians

in the Nigerian army 1956–66 had conformed to no established pattern. A period during which the speed of promotion had rapidly accelerated was followed by one in which it virtually came to a halt and the prospects for an individual in the middle seemed bleak. A young army may be operationally desirable, but it meant in Nigerian terms that those in the top posts had often not the experience to command respect for their high authority while those lower down were correspondingly frustrated. The fact that those in the upper echelons were in some cases disadvantaged by lack of education, being former Warrant Officers and NCOs, exacerbated the situation in a country where education and status were coming to be more and more closely associated. By comparison with this problem the fact that many NCOs were vastly more experienced than the officers with whom they had to work was relatively unimportant, partly because this was a situation recognized as normal in the British army. The situation was complicated by junior officers lacking the self-confidence to delegate to their NCOs and the fact that status distinctions of this kind did not fit in easily with the traditionally egalitarian patterns of many African communities. It should, however, not be forgotten that interrank tensions had been substantially alleviated in another way by the departure first of white NCOs and then of white officers. The way was at least open for the adaptation of the social arrangements to match traditional notions of reciprocal duty within an African tribal hierarchy.

An important consequence of rapid promotion on the scale experienced in the period from 1959 through to 1963 or 1964 was a kind of professional disorientation. This was noted in the Ghanaian as well as the Nigerian army and even those who benefited most in financial and status terms were known to express dissatisfaction at never being in any post sufficiently long to master the rôle and to become familiar with the tasks involved. Excessively rapid promotion undoubtedly creates false expectations and, more important, may affect the day-today judgment of the individuals concerned. Realism about practicable possibilities is particularly important in military situations, and progressive responsibility for larger- and larger-scale organizations over a short span of time can have a disorienting effect. In the Nigerian army promotion to major was most rapid for those commissioned in 1958–9: it was from this group that the conspirators of January 1966 mainly came. Did the speed of their promotion followed by the realization that further progress was blocked influence their participation? By contrast their juniors were in any case faced with a long wait for promotion, while their seniors had been through a much more orderly process. That none of the latter group was involved in the initiation of the coups of 1966 may have some significance.

It is arguable that factors related to the speed of promotion affected the stability of the army in other ways. The rotation of battalion commanders, for example, meant that one unit (the 5th Battalion) had four commanding officers in less than eighteen months. This was very unusual for any force outside wartime conditions, and may well have prevented the individual CO from establishing his authority, though in some senses it may have helped to unify the officer corps. The net effect was almost certainly to create a feeling of independence in the minds of unit officers who were on a day-to-day basis having to act without the constraints resulting from their superior's appreciation of their strengths, weaknesses and potentialities. In conditions of peace where the common purpose is hard to discern this may well have had a disintegrating and diverting effect. A lack of cohesion and a degree of irresponsibility were in these conditions almost inevitable.

Though the tribal, ethnic and regional aspects of the Nigerian situation can easily be exaggerated, they were certainly important factors in preventing the homogenization of military institutions in that country. There was a tendency for officers trained in Britain, in particular, to assert their loyalty to Nigeria while attributing tribal loyalties to others of different origin. This was a facet of the ambivalence which has already been remarked. The January plotters claimed to stand for 'one Nigeria'; the participants in the July coup asserted the danger to the nation of Ibo domination, and eventually the secession of Biafra was attempted on the grounds of escaping Northern domination.

There is little doubt that recruitment policies were both the product of and tended to confirm the trends of which the attitudes quoted were symptomatic. Other rank recruitment was established on a quota basis well before the end of British rule in rough proportions to the populations of the North, East and West. This was one factor which helped to make the census returns a major issue in Nigerian politics. The fact that recruitment from the Middle Belt was disproportionately large served only to weaken the notion of the army as an instrument of Moslem domination. The whole policy, which tended to treat the army as an educational institution promoting the spread of literacy rather than recruiting from the reservoir of those who were already literate, was a matter of contention between officers from different regions: those from the East virtuously proclaimed that the proper policy was to enlist the best quality of men – the best educated available – regardless of their origin. This was indeed what had begun to happen in the search for officers: the results were there for all to see in the shape of a dearth of men of Northern origin – where the level of literacy was generally lower – joining the commissioned ranks.

A regional officer recruitment quota was imposed in 1961 guaranteeing Northerners 50 per cent of the places for officer training in spite of the fact that this involved going well below the standard normally accepted in the qualifying examination. The Northern politicians and emirs were in practice claiming regional or even national needs as justification for the application of a double standard. The result was a tendency to make more consistent the character of the other rank and junior officer elements of the army which in turn was the overriding factor leading to the successful implementation of the counter-coup in July 1966. It effectively undermined criteria for entry to the profession by allowing an extraneous factor directly to influence selection. Henceforward respect for status in the hierarchy could be negated by the claims of regional allegiance.

During 1964 and 1965 the Nigerian army as a result became increasingly 'tribalized'. There were fears, hard to confirm, that a policy of rationalization involving compulsory retirement for middle ranking officers in order to break down the promotion block was to be introduced. The interpretation to be put by Eastern (or Western) captains and majors on this apparently sensible move was that it would be the act of a Northern minister of defence to further the careers and influence of his compatriots. Such fears have to be seen in the context of the exclusion of the East from power at the time by the North-West coalition, the suspicion of possible political interference in the army and the threat of its use to suppress what many felt to be legitimate political dissidence in the West especially after the allegations of a 'rigged election'. The actions of the Ironsi régime in relation to the army produced corresponding fears in other quarters, particularly when standards on officer-training courses were tightened up in such a way as to exclude some Northerners who had been accepted by the previous scheme under the quota system. It is evident that the problems of the military in administering Nigeria from January 1966 onwards were in part the product of their own development before and after independence, or, to put it another way, the Nigerian armed forces reflected the slowness of national progress towards political stability and an enduring unity.

The failure of the Ironsi administration in the face of a situation in which Ibo and Federal attitudes were already well on the way to total polarization does not in retrospect seem surprising. In January and February 1966 there was a sense of relief, as though Nigeria had been snatched back from a brink to which it had been led by the mutineers. At the same time the mistrust between the factions was so great that it is excusable to regard the catharsis of civil war as the only means of breaking it down. It would be hard to improve upon A. H. M. Kirk-Greene's summary of the position in his study of the Nigerian civil war:

> In the final analysis, the Nigerian tragedy has been bedevilled by a set of oppositions – generalized, stereotype, not necessarily of the same order and maybe imaginary, yet each widening the wound and reducing the hope of healing it: North v South, Islam v Christianity, alleged feudalism v assumed socialism, federal v unitary preferences, traditional authority v achieved elitism, haves v have-nots, each with sinister undertones of tension, irreconcilability and threatened withdrawal. None was entirely accurate. Nevertheless each opposing set had sufficient seed of truth within it to permit, and even fertilize, the growth of feared fact from the semi-fiction of its existence.*

If the military have in the longer term been responsible for bringing Nigeria to the point where these conditions no longer wholly apply then their achievement ought not to be belittled or at any rate wholly dismissed.

The kidnappings and murders in Lagos, Kaduna and Ibadan which had been accomplished by dawn on Saturday, 15 January 1966, had effectively destroyed one government but not put another in its place. The extent to which Major-General Ironsi had rallied loyalist elements in the army to check the coup leaders is not known, but the broadcast made at 2.30 p.m. from Lagos suggested that some steps must have been taken and that discussions were going on with a view to the formation of a military régime dedicated to national unity. The following day, Sunday, 16 January, the rump of the civilian cabinet

* A. H. M. Kirk-Greene, *Crisis and Conflict in Nigeria: A Documentary Sourcebook 1966-1969*, London, 1971, Vol. I, 5.

under the chairmanship of Zanna Bukar Dipcharima agreed without many preliminaries to hand over the government of the country temporarily to the army. Before midnight the Ironsi military government was announced and regional military governments responsible to the federal government were in process of being set up. Initially the success of Ironsi in securing the surrender of Major Nzeogwu and in designating Major Hassan Katsina as military governor of the North was reassuring and the general reactions to the new régime did not seem unfavourable. The disorders in the Western region which had been in a way the immediate cause of the crisis were quickly suppressed and the city of Ibadan, which had been threatened by anarchy, began to return to normal. Some bans on newspapers in the different regions were lifted and the firm hand was officially welcomed by the main political parties, by youth organizations, by trades unions whose political ineffectiveness had exacerbated matters, and by student bodies.

It is not clear how tenuous was the control of the Supreme Military Council in the first days of its existence, though it is doubtful if it was seriously threatened. The small group of conspirators quickly ceased to be a factor. Appropriate gestures were made with a view to restoring domestic confidence. There was, for instance, three days' official mourning for Sir Abubakar Tafawa Balewa, the murdered federal Prime Minister. At the same time the military government sought to reassure foreign interests by affirming its intention of honouring all treaty obligations and financial agreements. It intended to encourage foreign commercial and industrial enterprise and there would be no immediate further nationalization of industry and certainly none without full compensation. The new régime's intention was clearly to consolidate Nigeria's economic progress while seeking to unify the country and hopefully to probe the excesses which had led to corruption and in some areas to a deterioration of law and order.

The sets of opposites described by Kirk-Greene did, however, quickly reassert themselves. Relationships between the various groups within the army and the country at large rapidly deteriorated. Ironsi's deliberate attempt to match the personality and background of the regional governors to local needs and interests was in itself construed in some quarters as an open admission of the deep fissions affecting the state. Moreover, in spite of the somewhat adulatory acclaim of 'the simple soldier' which was a feature of the reporting, especially in Britain, of Ironsi's accession to power there were reasons for doubting whether his impartiality was sufficiently obvious. Few of those who had worked alongside him in the army doubted the reality of his Ibo allegiance; many questioned his efficiency and incorruptibility, others alleged that he was naïve and malleable. He was certainly, except for some romantic journalists, few people's image of the ideal soldier guardian. He had undoubtedly been at the centre of some of the sharper disputes relating to the regional balance within the army. It was he, as much as any other officer, who had advocated an open system of recruitment on the basis of educational achievement without regard for regional quotas. His views on this subject were well known as early as 1961, when they were interpreted by his critics as a disingenuous means of achieving Ibo supremacy. This had probably been at the root of the manoeuvring, said to originate with the now dead Sardauna of Sokoto, to prevent him from becoming Nigeria's first African GOC.

Whatever Ironsi's own attitudes and abilities, he was certainly not short of more radical advice from young officers in his entourage whose tribal affinities were in no sense concealed. Ojukwu was by now military governor in Enugu and altogether a more likely confidant for Ironsi than, for example, Hassan Katsina; the extent to which his undoubted intellectual ability was influential during this period, and in which directions, is still obscure. A comparison between Ironsi's failure to win the confidence of men from different regions and Yakubu Gowon's apparently exceptional success illustrates clearly not any inherent deficiencies in military government but the importance, in an entirely fortuitous way, of character and personality: this is a factor which studies of the military in politics have consistently neglected and which is in fact crucial. At the period in question the professionalism of the military and their personal relationships were not sufficient to offset the established divisive tendencies.

Quite apart from other practical considerations, the small size of the Nigerian armed forces led to the successive military governments relying heavily upon the civil service, especially the permanent secretaries in each ministry. The extent of their influence in determining policy was necessarily hard to judge. The obvious energy in the promotion of the economic life of the country of regional governors drawn from the armed forces has been a feature of Nigerian development since 1966; it is, however, unlikely, at least in the early stages, that they had any clear conception of a design for economic policy. However, one of the first moves of the Ironsi administration was to recall the heads of overseas missions to Lagos at the end of February 1966 for a briefing which significantly included visits to the Kainji Dam and to the Port Harcourt Oil Refinery as a demonstration of the high priority assigned to economic development. At the same time radical administrative reforms, especially of the national corporations, were being carried out and civil servants or technical experts were appointed to manage them. The influence of the military tradition itself was only obvious on a different plane. Like the Pakistan military before them, the regional governors in Nigeria displayed a quasi-puritanical obsession with efficiency simply conceived as, for example, punctuality. The governors of the Mid-West and Eastern regions, David Ejoor and 'Emeka' Ojukwu, both made an issue of the lack of promptness of civil servants in arriving at their desks by closing the doors of ministries at the opening hour of 8.0 a.m. and shaming the latecomers, of whatever rank, by making them queue outside where they were publicly harangued. Such actions helped to reinforce the popular impression of the military as patriotically dedicated to the public interest, as upright, honest, and concerned about waste of time and money. The same sort of thing happened under General Ankrah in Ghana.

There was perhaps less evidence in Nigeria of failure to grasp the merits of civil service procedures, seemingly because of a greater appreciation of the complexity of policy decisions. Nigerian civil servants readily accepted new responsibilities because they had not suffered the inhibiting effects of a dangerously authoritarian régime. The relative continuity of development even during the civil war demonstrated amongst other things the authority of the officials, and raised the important question whether vested interests against the revival of recognized political activity and a return to civilian rule were not in the process of generation.

From the first, apparently genuinely, Ironsi and his advisers endeavoured to prepare for a return to civilian rule. They set up study groups to consider a new constitution. Its particular form was not predetermined but Ironsi's overt preference was for a unitary state as not only his speeches but the actions of the régime implied. One evident possibility was for a presidential system on American lines: this might be more acceptable because it would open the doors to the selection of ministers from all walks of public life and make practicable the efficient deployment of the full reserve of talent in the national interest. This demonstrates the essential connection between the perceived rôle of a military administration and the notion of a national government acting in a crisis. There are signs of a parallel thinking on the part of the Gowon government in relation to 1976: the possibility of a radical constitutional innovation more appropriate to the needs of a rapidly developing state than conventional parliamentary democracy cannot be ruled out. Military rule would have served a useful purpose if a formula could be found which enabled full consultation and participation to be combined with efficient administration without the disruption and corruption seemingly inseparable from unleashing full-scale political rivalries.

Nigeria's search for a plausible alternative to military rule was affected in 1966, and presumably still is influenced, by two particularly important factors. In the first place, the Nigerian military are no exception to the general rule in preferring organizations in which there is a clearcut hierarchy, allocation and gradation of responsibility. The inherent differences of attitude between the main regions and peoples about the form of constitution which would best protect their interests in their turn, however, probably necessitate subtle checks and balances and, therefore, work against an uncomplicated system. The substitution of these for authoritarian control, however lightly exercised, is the central issue which has faced soldiers who are in power but are not altogether unwilling to return to barracks if the route could be found. In Nigeria after the first coup the federal and regional governments acted in such a way as at least to give the appearance of impartiality. In the Eastern region, for example, the drive against corruption involved the charging of a former regional Minister of Town Planning for 'corruptly accepting' £7500 and a Volkswagen car. On 5 March 1966 Dr Michael Okpara and nine of his political associates were placed in detention. Correspondingly, Hassan Katsina as Military Governor declared himself to be against the previous government's policy of 'northernization' and claimed that anyone from any part of Nigeria could get a job in the North. There was also talk of a uniform educational system for Nigeria which in the long run would have helped to eliminate some of the inter-regional anomalies.

Ironsi's dilemma was how to reconcile the ideas of 'one Nigeria', national unity and a strong central government with the local loyalties and sensitivities especially of Northerners. The Terms of Reference of the Constitutional Review Group*

* Kirk-Greene, *op cit.*, Vol. I, 158–9.

were in themselves matter-of-fact and unobjectionable, but in a speech at the opening session in March 1966 the Supreme Commander of the military government contrived to give the impression that that government was already committed to a unitary state and anxious to dismantle the cumbersome regional structure without being willing to take direct responsibility for such a decision. Suspicious minds almost certainly made more of this than was reasonable. The military government was caught between the requirements of consultation and the advantages of clearcut decision quickly implemented.

The difficulties during the first half of 1966 may have been ominously increasing but a dispassionate observer could claim that in a number of respects there were achievements which reflected the classic virtues of military administration. There was, for example, a period of three months or so when Nigeria was largely free of the violent disorders which were threatening to become endemic. Only disturbances in the area of the Niger Delta led by Isaac Boro and some banditry in the North and West marred the effectiveness of the army and the police in establishing the authority of the régime over a very large country. At the same time a level of newspaper criticism and political discussion was tolerated which was, to say the least, unusual in a period of army rule. There was an initial welcome for gestures aimed at ending the exploitation of power and corruption and the immediate tendency to fission seemed to have been halted. In fact, however, the traumatic effect of the murders of 15 January had yet to be felt. There was a relative lack of immediate emotional reaction to the announcements of the deaths, especially of the Sardauna and Sir Abubakar, but subsequent events revealed the true depth of feeling in the North. Without needing to attribute any bad motives to them, it could be said that General Ironsi and other key figures underestimated the task of dispelling suspicion which rested on their shoulders and even that, if they did fully appreciate the fact, they were unable to do much about it.

There was in fact infinite scope for 'small' men and fanatics to foster suspicion in private and public places. In these circumstances the obliteration of the widely-held belief that the army's intervention in politics amounted to a simple assertion of Ibo aspirations was an impossible task unless the supreme military council by some miracle was able to handle the affairs of the Northern region with such delicacy as to convince all those who mattered of its good intentions. The best hope lay in the wise appointment of Colonel Hassan Katsina as Military Governor and with it an assumed reliance on the vestiges of military cameraderie between officers trained in the same tradition. It is reasonable to suppose that the long telephone calls between 'Jack' and 'Emeka' – Gowon and Ojukwu – helped to postpone the attempt to gain independence for Biafra; in the same way, the Supreme Commander and his military governors may have been kept from open dissension as a result of their similar backgrounds and friendships formed during training. This 'military camaraderie' was in a sense, however, a double-edged weapon, as in some quarters it was felt that professional friendship and 'the old boy net' might prejudice the governors and impair their ability to protect regional interests.

The military régime did, however, assist the civil service, already well-trained and established at independence, to recover its morale. The Northern element might be wary of plans for unification of the service, but there was now an opportunity for a more or less fresh start with some relief from corruption and factional pressures. Senior civil servants faced with a welcome political moratorium soon assumed a policy-making rôle. The link between the problem of national unity and the promotion of a sound economy was perceived. The possibility of saving £26m. by dismantling the apparatus of regional government was tempting. The improvement in the balance of payments, already achieved in spite of the political confusion in 1965, increasing oil production, the rise of secondary industry and a sympathetic attitude on the part of the World Bank did, however, combine to assist the stability of the military régime. These favourable factors in themselves were not in the event sufficient to win the government the consensus of support it so badly needed: only the incentive of substantial wage increases could do that and this a military administration committed to austerity was in no position to provide.

It cannot be said that Ironsi's short-lived government made any unique policy innovations. The initial mild optimism about its prospects derived primarily from the balance of personalities and the Supreme Commander's personal authority over the young majors who had engineered the coup. The inherent possibility of inter-generational conflict within the army had no time to emerge because Ironsi had effectively canalized Nzeogwu's revolutionary initiative into more or less conventional channels. The rumours which soon circulated of a Nasser emerging to supersede Ironsi's Neguib were in the event only portents of what might have been had the régime survived. It is idle now to speculate about the emergence of more radical leadership within the original framework: had an Ibo challenger to Ironsi emerged he could only have precipitated the kind of Northern reaction which in any case occurred.

Studies of the military in African politics have habitually underplayed the unpredictable factor of personality: its contribution to the Nigerian dénouement is, however, indisputable. Ironsi, Gowon, Ojukwu – the succession of characters tells much of the story. The performance of Nigeria's current military administration is substantially attributable to the survival of Gowon. In 1966 Ironsi's amiable commonsense was insufficient in the face of the complexity of forces at work and the comparative sophistication of the political thought of some of the other participants. The regional administrations under their respective military governors tended to go their own way. Colonel Ojukwu, for example, emerged as an outspoken critic of tribalism. In May 1966 he decreed that all references to tribes be expunged from official documents in the Eastern region. No account was to be taken of place of origin in making public appointments. Nigerians must be allowed to live and work anywhere in the country without restriction. He had already ensured that competition for scholarships was related only to residence and not to parentage. This virtuous and possibly innocent insistence on a national principle was, however, as ever seen by Northerners as hypocritical and as a Machiavellian plot to consolidate Ibo influence in the public service and incidentally to win international sympathy.

In May 1966 the military government announced that it would not seek to retain office for longer than three years, but at the same time it barred all political parties and tribal organizations. Suspicions that this ban was a disingenuous means of prolonging military rule were almost certainly unwarranted. Political activity by tribal societies was at a level which mitigated against the achievement of reasonable stability before a return to civilian rule. The military government was at the turning point between acting as a holding administration and transforming itself into a government with a capacity for formulating policy over a given period. On the one hand were the senior civil servants poised to assume ministerial responsibilities, on the other was a range of public opinion deprived of the established party channels of communicating in any way with the central source of power. The Nigerian army, because of its small size in a large country, was not well known or naturally trusted. The banning of political activity and the promotion of a unitary state without strong regional groupings diminished the prospects of local popular· consultation and were only partially offset by the continued and notable freedom of the press and limited and somewhat erratic activity by the trades unions.

In several respects General Ironsi's radio broadcast of 23 May 1966 was a turning point. The details of a national development plan, remarks on food prices, university provision and rent control were completely overshadowed by the appearance

which he gave of formally announcing the termination of the
federal structure and of setting the seal on unitary government.
The fact that this was only a logical projection of what had
already been clearly implied was immaterial. It is not certain
even now that a unitary arrangement of the kind indicated was
intended to extend beyond the three-year period of military
rule. Indeed Hassan Katsina, the Northern Military Governor,
whether out of loyalty or otherwise, was at pains to relate the
proposal to normal military practice: 'We in the army have got
a unified command and it is the method we are used to. Such a
constitutional scheme would,' he assured a gathering of traditional rulers, 'not necessarily apply when civilian rule is
restored.' Every effort was made to present the arrangements
as temporary and provisional and essentially linked to the 'cor-
rective' rôle of the military government.

Sincerity and good intentions were, however, insufficient to
prevent the impending tragedy. A weekend of riots in the North
followed the speech. Disillusioned and frustrated politicians
provoked by the fading prospect of an early return to power
and the access which it provided to opportunities for the accumulation of wealth were apparently not slow to exploit the
prevalent intertribal, anti-Ibo tension. Advocacy of secession
by the North and of a referendum on a new constitution
seemed no more than a cover for cruder sentiments. More than
ninety people were reported killed, the majority of them in
Kano: there, the *Sabon Gari* or 'strangers' quarter' had been
cordoned off by the army to prevent further attacks on Ibos.
Once again the Military Governor endeavoured to calm the
situation less by his declared willingness to impose martial law
should it become necessary than by a reasoned defence of the
military government's proposals. He stressed the intention to
ensure fair representation of the regions in the government and
the administration, if necessary by boosting the development
of less developed areas, presumably especially in the field of
education. But he was faced with a depth of distrust about the

intentions of the Lagos government such as was incapable of
reduction. He nevertheless persisted with his conciliating rôle
even when the disorders spread to his father's emirate of
Katsina, reiterating the views that no permanent constitutional
changes were being introduced, that civil service operations
would retain a local flavour and that crash education and training programmes would benefit the Northern provinces.

In June the military government announced that it would
undertake to organize a referendum on the changes which in
any case were only designed to facilitate administration by a
unified military command. This step, fully publicized by the
government at the national and regional level, was too late: the
flight of Ibos from the North was already in progress and the
upward spiral of suspicion and threat accelerating.

From the point of view of preserving peace and stability the
steps taken after mid-June to deal with corruption, land
speculation and abuse of public office were largely irrelevant.
In July the military government recognized the vacuum in
communications created by its proscribing of political activity
and implicitly its own isolation from the trends of opinion, by
convening a meeting in Ibadan of local rulers from all parts of
Nigeria. The possibility that the chiefs had a political as well as
an administrative rôle to play had to be faced and the Nigerian
government was not alone in Africa in at least subconsciously
recognizing this consequence of its own establishment. In the
event, however, the Ibadan meeting was the occasion of
General Ironsi's last public appearance. On the following night,
Ibo officers and men were attacked at Ibadan, Abeokuta, Ikeja
and Kaduna. It was this that led Ojukwu to suggest from Enugu
that 'the brutal and planned annihilation of officers of Eastern
Nigerian origin' had cast serious doubt on the possibility of the
peoples of Nigeria living together as one nation. Indeed the
rebels themselves were reported as demanding the secession of
the West and the North as the Kano rioters had done in May.
It was at this point that the young Colonel Yakubu Gowon

assumed control following Brigadier Ogundipe's refusal to take command. The proposed unitary structure of government had focussed and magnified the distrust which had already been brought to a head by the January coup. The army had failed to end the domination of Nigerian politics by tribalism and in so doing had come near to totally destroying itself.

Ironsi's activities as Supreme Commander, whatever his personal qualities and defects, were prejudiced from the start by the failure to convince the mass of the population that the national image officially presented was genuine. A lenient attitude to the original mutineers was automatically construed as condonation of, if not complicity in, the murders of 15 January. Thenceforward each step towards the reformation of government and the civil service was misinterpreted. Northerners, always ready to see themselves at a competitive disadvantage in the public service, revived and refurbished the old stories of intertribal hatred and atrocity. In its turn the murder of many Ibos between July and October 1966 made a secession by 'Biafra' and, therefore, civil war virtually inevitable. It was the Ibos' turn to generate atrocity stories and again there was enough evidence to make them fully credible to eager listeners.

The tragic progress towards the outbreak of war was not in itself a function of military intervention in politics. If anything, as has been already suggested, the existence of a military fraternity was a mildly restraining factor in that it provided a pretext for continued communication until the last. The first phase of Nigerian government had indicated the dangers of military personnel involving themselves in the general struggle for power within a society. The Ibo majors of the January coup saw themselves as Nigerian patriots but came quickly to be regarded as the champions of their own regional compatriots whose political power, for the time being, did not correspond with their socio-economic strength. The determination of the Northern leadership to retain overriding authority in the face of relative economic weakness and a shortage of educated

manpower constituted a challenge. The rebels saw no way
of changing the balance except by force. The consequences of
their actions are clear, because the Ironsi government's short-
lived claim to success lay in the attempt to suppress tribalism
and to shift power away from the North. In so doing it failed –
as was almost inevitable – to cope with the political realities,
and in failing it forced the Easterners into wanting for the first
time strong regions in a loose federation rather than a strong
central government based on a conglomeration of small states.
The true 'One Nigeria' of the rebels' aims was more remote than
ever.

There is no need here to trace the sad sequence of events
leading to the civil war: the deterioration in relations between
the federal government and its Eastern regional subordinate
was not attributable to strictly military considerations. The
rôle of personality was, however, important, and even more
significant if N. U. Akpan's* account of Ojukwu's rôle is taken
absolutely literally. A great deal has been written about the
subsequent conduct of the war. The question why it lasted so
long raised at the time some doubts about the capacity of the
Federal military régime in circumstances in which it appeared
to command overwhelming strength. Certainly some of its
commanders were more ruthless than others: perhaps many of
its soldiers had little enthusiasm for a war against fellow
Nigerians. Probably most significant were the special dedica-
tion of Biafrans to their cause and the formidable task of
the Federal administration in raising, training and arming so
large an army in so short a time. The devious activities of
external forces confused the issues, but in the end the federal
military government was left determined to resolve its own
problems.

The first of these was and perhaps remains the war machine
which it had created. Before it could concentrate on unifying

* *The Struggle for Secession 1966–1970: a personal account of the
Nigerian Civil War*, London, 1972.

and governing the country it had to try to reduce the army and some of its commanders to size. Salaries for ordinary soldiers as much as eight times the average Nigerian income and steady employment for men without previous experience had created a new vested interest. Demobilization would clearly create its own problems but at the same time indiscipline and desertion threatened the fabric of law and order such as it was. Gowon, by his conciliatory style, managed to avoid the worst dangers: the scattered formations did not take authority into their own hands, and his apparent disinclination to identify with and to control the individual commanders at the front now became something of a virtue. He was not the army's prisoner, nor enmeshed with the politicians. His generous treatment of the Biafran leadership, once Ojukwu had departed, seemed a strictly personal achievement, but one with far-reaching and beneficial consequences.

The possibility that more depends upon the character of the leader than on the military character of a régime is borne out in the case of Gowon as certainly, but entirely differently, as in the case of Amin. On most facets of Yakubu Gowon's character and conduct there has been a remarkable degree of agreement. He is generally believed to be a modest man who reluctantly accepted the responsibility of Head of State as a military duty and to possess generally the opposite qualities to those required for success in the Nigerian political jungle. His experience of life was largely confined to the artificial environs of the officers' mess where he was more noted for quiet efficiency than for charismatic qualities. The fact that he had made his mark at Sandhurst was attributable to his absorption of the appropriate ethos and of itself not by any means necessarily an asset amongst his African colleagues and contemporaries. Moreover, when he took office at the age of thirty-one he was the youngest head of state in the world; his inexperienced innocence was glaringly exposed at the Aburi talks in Ghana, where he attempted to avoid the declaration of Biafran secession, by

Ojukwu's sophisticated and carefully prepared presentation of his cause.

Few political leaders could in normal circumstances have survived being publicly outclassed to such a degree, but in this case subsequent events provide their own commentary. Ojukwu disappeared into exile in the Ivory Coast, while Gowon's achievement of reconciliation in Nigeria was followed up by an increase in his external stature culminating in one year, 1973, in unanimous election to chairmanship of the Organization of African Unity, the state visit to London and an effective presence at the Commonwealth Conference at Ottawa. The once – in African terms – dubious merits of his British training and cultural orientation had been converted into political assets enabling him to take a strong line on Rhodesia and South Africa. It was, however, the reunification of Nigeria after the civil war which established his reputation in Western eyes. Portentous prognostications of massacre and genocide of Ibos were nullified in the first instance by his example. 'There will be no Nuremberg trials,' he is reported to have declared. 'We will bind up the nation's wounds.' Some observers went so far as to claim that his was a policy of clemency and mercy unparalleled in recent history and one which even a corresponding European leader could not have attempted. His willingness to reabsorb Biafran rebels into the federal armed forces seemed the most remarkable aspect of his personal achievement. Not only were former opponents treated with magnanimity but he did not preclude the development of trust and loyalty on a personal level: his employment of Ibo pilots for his own plane might well have seemed foolhardy to some.

With the civil war over and a conciliatory atmosphere established, the military government faced a range of problems. In the first place it was necessary to re-establish the credibility of the régime in the management of the economy and international relationships. This proved less difficult than might have been predicted: on the whole, world and African continental conditions proved favourable to Nigeria, which after all was the largest state in the region and by no means devoid of natural resources. The peculiar internal problems of a military administration proved less obviously tractable. The enormous standing army of around two hundred thousand men left over from the war itself constituted a range of tests in the fields of law and order, employment and possible restraints on government expenditure. There was, in addition, the overriding question of the extent to which the government machine was to be controlled and directed by the military or whether the civil service was to play an increasing rôle in policy-making. Beyond these aspects was the possibility of some form of controlled return to civilian rule and the necessary preconditions for that.

The core of potential success for the military government lay in its ability to restrain a potentially dangerous army, to occupy it constructively and at the same time to encourage Ibo confidence. In less than two years Ibos were returning to the North to take up official positions. At the same time, in the East Central State, where Ukpabi Asika was civilian administrator, economic redevelopment was proceeding at a rapid rate in spite of the prevalence of armed robbery and some resistance to the payment of taxes. The identification of Asika with the federal cause was offset by the appointment to key rôles of former active protagonists of the Biafran cause, notably Dan Njemanze, formerly Ojukwu's Deputy Director of Military Intelligence, as Commissioner for Economic Development. Less well publicized was the nomination of Dr Ukwu I. Ukwu, a lieutenant-colonel in the Biafran army, as Commissioner for Trade and Industry and later for Finance. In similar vein, the University of Nsukka was reconstituted with many of its former staff, as well as other prominent ex-Biafrans, such as the famous novelist, Chinua Achebe, in the post of Director of the Institute of African Studies.

The behaviour of the Federal army after the war, notably of

the 1st division based in Enugu and under the command of
Colonel I. D. Bissala, went a long way towards reducing tensions. The handling of the cases of key Biafran officers was,
however, necessarily fraught with difficulty. The Commission,
set up after the war under the chairmanship of Colonel Robert
Adebayo to investigate their situation in relation to the Federal
army, considered the situation of more than 150 officers, and
attempted to establish shades of blame. There was in the end
little doubt that the decisions in a number of cases to detain
officers were influenced by sectional interests within the army,
from the Rivers State, the Mid-West and so on. No doubt the
true spirit of reconciliation would have drastically reduced
these still small figures but there were clearly limits to the
acceptable generosity. By way of contrast, the promotions of
senior officers David Ejoor, Ekpo, Hassan Katsina and
Adebayo to the rank of general were aimed at restoring a
proper, readily recognizable hierarchy and avoiding the inflammation of feelings which would have resulted had Colonel
Benjamin Adekunle been preferred. While reconciliation was
not always as thoroughgoing as was presented, or at any rate
did not seem so to Ibos, it is doubtful whether it could ever have
been attempted other than by a military régime led by so
restrained and apparently simple a man as Gowon.

The rationale of defence spending was less easily discernible.
The introduction of public executions for those convicted of
armed robbery confirmed that which was widely known, namely
the prevalence of serious crime. Some attributed the level of
criminality largely to the ready availability of weapons and to
the presence of undisciplined soldiers free to roam the country-
side. In mid-1971 the Federal Commissioner for Finance, Chief
Obafemi Awolowo, held defence expenditure responsible for the
£N 33 million increase in the 1971–2 budget. He suggested that
the military owed a duty to the economy and that soldiers be
employed in agriculture, building construction and road
making. The traditional hostility in the armed forces to the use

of their personnel on a large scale as labourers in 'normal' conditions prevailed: professional objections were reinforced by the fear of the consequences of effectively enabling the reflection of workers' grievances, and even trades union practices, within the military organization. There has in Nigeria been no lack of recognition of the socio-political dangers of the peaceful uses of military forces. The question of defence expenditure, therefore, remained a sore point. There was even some suspicion that the public uncertainty about the real size of the armed forces was due to a need to justify expenditure which in the period 1969-71 appeared to run at two to three times the estimated figure. For example, actual expenditure in the six months 1 April to 30 September 1970 was £N 61·73 million as compared with £N 21·91 million during the same period in 1969 when the Biafran war was still continuing. The difference did not appear to be accounted for by the estimates relating to the construction of new barracks to house a permanent, peacetime force.

Not only was the unresolved problem of the size of the standing army affecting domestic priorities in public expenditure and creating suspicion and discontent. The aftermath of war in the shape of delayed payments for foreign weapons and equipment, and the cost of rehabilitating a rapidly recruited force, was a serious drain on foreign currency. Only concern for economic development, especially the exploitation of oil resources, masked a serious dilemma typical of the military in power.

The attitude of the Gowon administration to economic policy was most clearly demonstrated in the promulgation of the Second National Development Plan in November 1970. This plan asserted among its many objects greater Nigerian control over the national destiny and the effecting of social change. The need for national unity was stressed and to this end the provision of road communications, water supply and electricity to people in less favoured areas was to take priority. Capital expenditure on agriculture was to be increased and the plan recognized, without attempting to resolve in detail, the obstacles laid in the way of an agrarian revolution by local systems of land tenure. The sensitivity of the government to traditional interests was recognized to the point of declining to take official action: the military, as much as any civilian government, were hampered by the conflict between the economic need for large-scale farming and land as the foundation of social security in the extended family sense. The implications and potentialities of its own creation, the National Agricultural Bank, were shirked. On the other hand, firm control was assumed over the question of industrial location, and the educational provisions set out to bridge the development gap between the states as well as to make up the undoubted deficiency of intermediate-level personnel. Parochialism in the recruitment of skilled labour was seen as an obstacle to the efficient use of resources and also to the vaguely asserted aim of full employment. The need to control, not necessarily by legal ownership, the vital natural resources of the country was balanced by the concept of economic integration with Nigeria's neighbours. It is arguable that in the implementation of this worthy plan too much power was given to state governors and their officials, who, though they helped to create an often productive inter-state rivalry, were not always aware of the national strategy. Given the many obstacles, including persistent corruption, military personnel may be said to have contributed a certain dynamism to the Nigerian economy since the civil war.

It is primarily her economic dynamism, combined with the obvious fact of size, which has provided since 1970 the basis for a new initiative in Nigeria's external relations, especially within the OAU. There had been earlier attempts to establish her primacy by seeking the post of Secretary-General for Nigeria and so on. It was, however, only after the civil war that the federal government adopted a more positive line for the fostering of African unity. No longer were principles pursued to the

point where compromise was impossible: statesmanlike intervention, as in the question of Ugandan representation at OAU
meetings after the Amin coup, became the order of the day.
Reconciliation with those four African states that had recognized 'Biafra' was quickly effected. Nigeria's Foreign Minister,
Dr Okoi Arikpo, forcefully promoted the notion of a common
African policy on international issues. The military government, realizing the advantages which it had derived during the
war from the large measure of OAU solidarity, sought to maintain this by establishing the legitimacy of the Organization on
the basis of its majority decisions.

The corollary of African solidarity was from Nigeria's standpoint a greater involvement in the campaign for the elimination
of colonialism from Africa which the pre-1966 government had
kept in low key. Portuguese, South African and Rhodesian
support for 'Biafra' was an important incentive to greater involvement, a more substantial financial commitment to the
OAU Liberation Committee and direct aid to 'freedom fighters':
control and direction of the campaign would also be an important weapon in Nigeria's hands for a number of purposes.
Even so the establishment of some kind of co-ordinated military
command proved impossible when discussed at the Rabat
summit in 1972.

On the economic front co-operation was towards less sen-
sational but in many ways more practical ends. In April 1972
General Gowon and President Eyadema of Togo signed a treaty
which established the basis of a West African Economic Community. A feature of General Gowon's attitude has been an
overt awareness of the inhibiting effects of the residual commercial and financial arrangements between Francophone
countries. His personal intervention probably affected the
character of the arrangements established at Bamako in June
1972 for a *Communauté Économique de l'Afrique Occidentale*
(CEAO). Similarly, public criticism in Nigeria of associate
status with the EEC has influenced the whole question of the

Community's relationship with Africa. Trade agreements and actual trade with other African states were greatly extended and by 1972 Nigeria had formal arrangements with over 25 African countries as compared with 9 in 1966. Alongside this was an extension of aid to the weaker states like Malawi, Lesotho and Botswana: Nigerian experts in some cases replaced European expatriates. A grant of aid to Dahomey, interest-free, for the reinstatement of the Porto Novo–Nigerian border road was the first of its kind and at least partly attributable to the principle of reducing dependence on Europe and other outside sources.

Nigeria had even before 1966 initiated an active line of support for OAU intervention in the settlement of inter-state disputes in Africa. The Gowon régime carried this policy several stages further by advocating that not only all international disputes but also major internal problems should be resolved through OAU machinery in order to avoid foreign exploitation of such issues. The unsuccessful attempt to settle the Uganda–Tanzania dispute in 1971 by this means was significant in that during the 1960s Nigeria had consistently regarded such interventions as contrary to the OAU charter. Correspondingly, resistance to the involvement of the United Nations in African disputes mounted. All this coincided with the cultivation of active Nigerian leadership in OAU affairs.

The interesting question was how far the growth of Nigerian determination was due to the momentum generated by increased military and economic strength and how far to a positive ideology on the part of the military leadership. Certainly their success in re-establishing unity at home enhanced the country's international status. Economically the rise in the annual growth rate to 12 per cent by 1972 and the doubling of the foreign monetary reserves in the corresponding two-year period provided the base. It was almost certainly the unparalleled growth in foreign investment in Nigeria at the beginning of the 1970s and her emergence as probably the most rapidly expanding market in Africa which gave her the strength and the prestige to press for a substantial increase in contributions by OAU members to the special fund of the Liberation Committee as well as to start helping her needy neighbours.

A stronger Nigeria involved necessarily greater foreign commitment to her future and this in turn led to an increase in Nigerian influence outside the African continent. Britain, for example, tended to become more sensitive to Nigerian opinion about Rhodesia and South Africa and it was probably at least a covert belief in Africa that British and American support for the white-dominated régimes could be eroded: this may well have consolidated General Gowon's personal position as the man most likely to be able to exert effective diplomatic pressure. The expansion of the armed forces was another factor which helped to convince Nigerian leaders that the time was ripe for a more active rôle in the 'liberation' of the remaining colonies and white-dominated territories in Africa, which were in any case, as already suggested, regarded as partly responsible for the prolongation of Biafran resistance. In an address at the OAU summit meeting in September 1969 General Gowon referred to the plots to divide Nigeria and said, 'We have no choice but to commit ourselves wholly to the struggle against racial oppression.' Liberation was a prerequisite to real economic development. Moreover, the OAU had, by its diplomatic support for the federal government during the Civil War, established itself firmly in the eyes of the Nigerian leaders. Respect for the articles of the OAU Charter dealing with non-interference in the affairs of other states was also a guarantee to weaker states who might in the future feel threatened by a neighbouring giant.

Whereas in its external and development function the specific rôle of the military in the Nigerian state apparatus is necessarily indistinct as compared, for example, with that of the civil service and other civilians, who might in other circumstances have been political leaders, in the matter of the future character of the Nigerian government its rôle is critical and distinct. The method and precise timetable of the return to civilian rule were still in 1974 unresolved and the future beyond 1976 is unclear. How what could be regarded as the last stage in reconciliation and reconstruction is to be achieved remains uncertain, and, not surprisingly in the circumstances, there have been few voices openly suggesting that the goal might not be civilian political rule in its conventional form. The twelve-state system proved the salvation of Nigeria, even though in the first instance it precipitated attempted secession, and their effective consolidation remains central to the building of modern Nigeria. Gowon's popularity in some quarters derives from the magnanimity, which as a Christian from a Northern minority group, he was able to show to the defeated Ibos. His achievement has been described as comparable only with that at the end of the American civil war. Reconciliation essentially took the form of encouraging Ibos to play key rôles in the re-construction of the East Central State, and facilitating their employment in specialist rôles in other states. In relation to population Iboland was, in Nigerian terms, overpopulated with skilled men. The restoration of Ibo property acquired by invest-ment in other parts of the country was also important for the restoration of morale. The twelve state units of growth and activity created healthy economic competition and at the same time fragmented old political rivalries.

The task of designing a new political game is likely to prove more fundamental than in other countries which have experi-enced military rule. The suppression of political activity did not mean that Nigeria ceased to be political; economic develop-ment was bound to generate fresh political interests and alliances. Events in Ghana with its second military government were carefully noted and might contribute to a long postpone-ment of a real transfer of power. Even so, the special character-istics of a military government which has had to rely exten-sively on civil servants are not easy to distinguish. The large armed forces after the civil war were not obviously obtrusive; for instance, they directed traffic during the changeover from the left to the right-hand side of the road. Individual military state governors adopted typically the 'spot' first-hand inspection of their regions as though they were battalions in training and thereby usefully acquired a reputation for intimacy with the problems of the people at the grass-roots level. The eventual conversion of some of them into the political leaders of the future was not unlikely. Meanwhile the press and the judiciary maintained a degree of independence with results not always agreeable to the military government. At the same time a faith in General Gowon's word about an end to strictly military rule in 1976 generally prevailed, but the procedures to be adopted were complicated by the complex constitutional issues arising from the twelve-state system. The revenue allocation from federal to state governments depended at least in part on the organization of an effective and acceptably accurate census. States varied in their degree of financial dependence on Lagos for development finance. There was, however, at heart a healthy and realistic realization of the importance of the steps to be taken from reconciliation and unity to a long-term political stability.

As early as 1970 General Gowon appointed 1976 as the target date for a return to civilian rule. He provided a clear-cut programme enumerating the measures necessary. The implementation of the National Development Plan 1970–4 was for all reasonable purposes carried out by 1974, though problems remained in the establishment of an agricultural system appropriate to a large modern state. The reorganization of the army (and its permanent housing) was a more difficult and controversial question: the cost and socio-political implications of a force of more than 200,000 men was not seriously questioned perhaps because safe means of running it down could not be devised. The drafting of a new constitution was slow to begin and there was a strong impression that the military government felt that radical change was unnecessary in that the central authority could control state activity by financial allocations. The importance attached to the census – first results of which were due to be published in March 1974 – suggested a proper concern for the availability of reliable data for planning and at the same time perhaps a subconscious need to focus on aspects irrelevant to the real problems of the transfer of power. General Gowon's own emphasis on 'free and fair elections', 'properly elected governments' and 'genuinely national parties' raised questions without giving the slightest indication as to their solution; similarly with the 'eradication of corruption'.

By the beginning of 1974, if not earlier, the point had been reached where enthusiasm for the 1976 deadline was in question not so much because a return to civilian rule was an objective to be abandoned, but because in general the mass of Nigerians were less concerned about the continuance of military government than the Military Government themselves. This was likely, if true, to have been due to the image of a régime represented in popular eyes at least as often by civilian commissioners, civil servants and heads of statutory bodies as by soldiers or policemen. This suggested a respect for and acceptance of Gowon's government which, if it manifestly declined as a result of the government's retention of power beyond an appropriate date, might threaten its achievement most by creating tensions within the armed forces themselves. The controversy which arose in June 1973 over an address by Allison Ayida, Permanent Secretary of the Ministry of Finance, stressing the influence of himself and his civil service colleagues in policy-making, indicated that a kind of power struggle was in any case going on in Nigeria within the nominally military structure. The artificiality of deliberate steps to an elusive notion of civilian rule was emerging as a possible lesson from the complexity of the Nigerian experience. In the event General Gowon announced on 1 October 1974 the formal abandonment of the plan to return to civilian rule by 1976. And on 29 July 1975 Gowon was himself deposed.

VI · Mobutu's Zaïre 1965-74

The case of Zaïre (formerly the Belgian Congo and then Congo (Kinshasa)) demonstrates more clearly than any other in Africa not only the difficulties inherent in attempting to categorize types of military intervention in politics, but the problem of defining a military régime. For Zaïre has been since 1965 at any rate very much the kingdom of General Joseph Mobutu. Under his management the penetration of normally civilian functions, at whatever level, by military officers has been negligible and a single party programme has been established within which Mobutu himself has been the only soldier to have official status in the party 'politbureau'. No official consideration appears to have been given to a return to civilian rule in the strict sense. Instead, via a presidential election and the party system, a new basis for the legitimacy of the existing régime has been sought. Mobutu has also sought to limit the opportunities for personal civil power within the party, while consolidating his own position by ensuring that the army is controlled by ethnically and otherwise reliable personnel in all the garrisons within one day's drive of the capital, Kinshasa.

Mobutu's régime in its lasting form dated effectively from 24 November 1965 when, after the popular rebellions of 1964-5, Mobutu and the Armée Nationale Congolaise (ANC) High Command unseated the two rivals for the presidency, Moise Tshombe and Joseph Kasavubu, and proclaimed a state of emergency. From that time onwards Mobutu was in personal control not so much as a military dictator but as the head of a skilfully manipulated bureaucracy made up of diverse ethnic and social groups. His achievement in establishing the necessary bureaucratic hierarchy with the relevant rules and conventions was remarkable: the maintenance of a personally centralized system necessarily involved arbitrary control over the careers and status of individuals. It also required a high degree of secrecy as well as an appreciation of the range of interests within the class structure and for this reason detailed evidence as to its operation remains hard to come by.

Mobutu's government sought to demonstrate its technical expertise and it was characteristic of such a structure that a rational/pragmatic approach to economic problems was largely unhindered by external political factors. For example, the practical convenience and advantages of cultivating the American and not unrelated Israeli connections in the commercial and industrial fields were initially obvious; it was logical to co-operate with Taiwan at the same time. However, when General Mobutu, during 1972, appreciated the radical nature of the change in US attitudes towards Peking he was apparently indignant that he had not been forewarned and his reaction was characteristically pragmatic. The former target of Peking radio, which accused him of being 'an American imperialist lackey', went off to China in January 1973, negotiated a trade agreement and established full diplomatic relations. China's earlier support for the rebel movement led by Mulele was quickly relegated to the background. It is probable that both parties saw financial advantage in allowing China direct access to Zaïre's mineral resources, thus bypassing the capitalists in the shape of the London Metal Exchange for the purchase of raw materials. Zaïre's immediate reward was the offer of a $100 million loan for agricultural development.

Initially – and especially in speeches made during December 1965 – Mobutu emphasized economic needs: he stressed the catastrophic decline in agricultural production, the rise in prices and general inflation. He diverted funds from prestige projects such as dams and ironworks to basic agriculture. Like many military leaders before and since, including Colonel Acheampong in Ghana and even General Amin in Uganda,

Mobutu involved people of all categories and classes in actions of domestic economy like street cleaning in order to identify the people with a drive for patriotic emotional commitment. All state officials were required to cultivate at least two-and-a-half acres of land. Steps were taken to ensure that graduates made a proper contribution to national development by a period of teaching. The predominant characteristic of his régime, which resembled Mussolini's Italy more than the more ruthless authoritarian states, was the establishment of a range of agencies to co-ordinate development of all kinds and, for example, to improve distribution of food stuff.

Even more than most military rulers, Mobutu despised politicians and regarded the army as the national depository for moral rectitude. He accused the politicians since independence in 1960 of wrecking the country by their sordid intrigues and personal rivalries while ignoring the welfare of the people. For the first five years political parties were banned, though Mobutu's own Popular Revolutionary Movement (MPR) was allowed to continue on the somewhat spurious basis that it was a nationalist movement not a political party and as such opposition was clearly not tolerable. The new constitution of 1967 gave Mobutu, as President for seven years in the first instance, full authority to operate a presidential-style government in which all senior public servants were personal appointments and the distinction between ministers and civil servants was arbitrary. The dissolution of Parliament in 1967 meant, for Mobutu's purpose, only the abandonment of the democratic façade which it provided, for he had used it only to reinforce his own constitutional position and to control the bureaucracy. The effect of this step was to make clearer to all concerned the chain of command and to establish rules effectively inhibiting the kind of political volatility which had prevailed before 1965 and which was to an extent typical of other African states.

In economic terms Mobutu's essentially pragmatic approach certainly bore fruit. The stabilization of the currency seemed to relate directly to the onset of prosperity. Agricultural production quickly exceeded the best pre-independence level. Expenditure, especially on public employees, was still mounting but this was offset by the rising world price of minerals, especially copper. The prosperity enjoyed under Mobutu's government was appreciated most by the already privileged elements of officialdom in all its forms, military and civilian: consciously or unconsciously those interests most likely to pose a threat to the régime were cultivated by financial inducements.

The history of the Congo since independence did, however, indicate that the General's main preoccupation, if he sought long-term stability, must be to create a structure which would prevent a resurgence of tribal activity. To this end, after an interval he reduced the numbers of provinces from twenty-one, many of them recently created, to twelve: the necessary elections and appointments were tightly supervised. In certain key areas army officers had already temporarily taken over the administration contrary to Mobutu's quickly established principle of not employing the army in the normal functions of government. This was apparently the first step towards the early realization of Mobutu's complete control over the functioning of the provincial administrations. This stage lasted much less than a year and at the end of December 1966, in the face apparently of continued political dissidence by minorities, the further reduction of the provinces to eight amounted almost to a restoration of the pattern which had prevailed during the colonial period. These provinces were in future to be administered rather than governed; the representative assemblies became advisory bodies and officials were deliberately transferred to areas far away from their places of origin. The alleged tendency of military régimes to restore the forms and relationship of colonial rule was thus classically demonstrated. The move had the advantage of further eliminating the opportunities available for exploitation by shifts in political loyalty, the inclinations to which were illustrated by the Kisangani mutiny and dismissals from office during 1967. The policy of appointing locally impartial officials involved a major upheaval in the lives of many of them and there was naturally some resistance. Nevertheless, the financial corruption which had arisen through personal links between officials and contractors was at any rate temporarily undermined.

It might be argued that one of Mobutu's shrewdest moves was to mobilize the educated élite. In particular he created a Presidential Advisory Board to serve as a kind of personal 'think-tank' drawn from products of Lovanium University. By 1968 more than half the key posts in the Cabinet were held by graduates. In a country where such manpower was at independence in 1960 in acutely short supply, their mobilization to serve the new state was from authority's point of view a masterly stroke.

So tightly effective was General Mobutu's new type of control that the chances of a far-reaching successful conspiracy seemed to have been almost eliminated. This security was, however, gained at the obvious expense of the profits derived from a free exchange of views and inhibited initiative and discretion by the simple means of strictly limiting the availability of information. Typically this involved the development of a small, tightly-related group around the President, including a secret service organization directly responsible to him as well as a cadre of envoys for deployment on overseas or internal missions of a delicate kind. It appeared that these arrangements were not wholly the product of spontaneous reaction to practical problems. The Ministry of Information in fact issued a document, *From Legality to Legitimacy*, which was in the form of a manifesto signed by Mobutu himself. Its message is plain – there is a clear distinction between those public issues on which the population is able and entitled to make judgments and those on which only an expert élite is qualified to express an opinion. The inference is clearly that the functioning of that élite is the direct responsibility of the President, an office identified with Mobutu.

Progressively, and in keeping with the philosophy expressed in this document, the military character of the régime faded. The emphasis was on the personality of Mobutu who himself tended to discard army uniform: there were indeed some parallels with the overt civilianization stage of the Nasser administration in Egypt. Mobutu seemed consciously to appreciate the need to avoid identification with any particular interest group in the country, uniformed or otherwise. While using his knowledge of the army acquired in the ranks to continue to consolidate his personal security, he seemed to conclude that the most important requirement was to prevent civilians with popular appeal from exercising it in key posts. Only this could account for the exceptionally rapid rate of turnover in Cabinet posts. Many ministers were exiled after a short period of office for no apparent reason. Men like Victor Nendaka, who had worked with Mobutu from independence onwards, were demoted and then removed from office with varying degrees of speed.

Though the Mobutu government has been in many respects unique in Africa, its attitude to foreign relations from the first conformed to that of the more usual pattern of conservative military régimes. The international honour of the state was emphasized. The Congo had to be seen as taking initiatives when the opportunity offered. With this went a national sensitivity to real or imagined slights, well illustrated by incidents in the developing relationship with Britain, and the heavy cost of ceremonial receptions for foreign visitors, including a luxurious new palace outside Kinshasa. One problem was to reconcile the colourful apparatus of a dictatorship with the essential cultivation of popular support. Apart from the identification of suitable scapegoats, such as white mercenaries, and the occasional successful ceremonial progress round the country, the procedure of the constitutional referendum was used as a means of identifying regional dissent and taking action to deter it. Care was taken to emphasize the characteristically national-ist aspects of the régime by denying its connection with or derivation from any foreign ideology – capitalist or communist. The mode of address '*citoyen*' was officially adopted and Mobutu was regarded as the particular custodian of the revolu-tionary spirit or ethos.

How far the philosophy and rationale of the so-called 'Congo-lese Revolution' was the work of one man is hard to judge. The evidence for crediting Mobutu himself with many subtle and deliberate acts is not slight but almost entirely circumstantial. His efforts to achieve the unlikely combination of support from university students and the growing middle class suggested a facility to divert at least one of the groups from their true socio-economic interests – at any rate for the time being. At the same time he banked on the army's painful recollections of its previous incarnation as the colonial *Force Publique* just after independence to keep it generally out of politics. He was not always successful, but was at pains to conceal evidence of surges of discontent within the ANC to the point of conspiracy. It was evident that in October 1966 the High Command, in spite of Mobutu's protestations to the contrary, did pressurize Mobutu into dismissing General Mulamba from the post of Prime Minister and immediately from the consolating niche of Minister of National Defence, to which he was transferred. The same body seems also to have dissuaded the General in 1968 from granting an amnesty in the case of Pierre Mulele, the leader of the rebellion in Kwilu province. Mobutu had himself very largely been responsible for forging a 'new model army' purged of corruption and more consciously hierarchical than before. The ANC was, however, beginning to experience the usual problems of a military inter-generational conflict caused by the training of many younger officers overseas.

To some extent Mobutu's success in consolidating popular support was a matter of political good fortune. Socially conscious youth movements already existed before his access to power, and his determination to avoid factional commitment enabled them to be consolidated into one national body. At the same time the university students responded to the opportunities which his régime provided to reflect their militant nationalism as well as apparently appreciating the scope available in an apparently technocratic administration. This was sufficient to compensate for the continuance of poor financial and material provision while at university.

Fortuitously, the economic policies of the government also encouraged indigenous business enterprise on a large scale without seriously threatening foreign investment. The state intervened in attempting to bring down food prices but was also concerned with the prestige aspects of retail trade in the shape of a luxury department store. In terms of state ownership the crisis came with Union Minière's determination to control the price of copper exports unilaterally, but on the whole Mobutu did not commit himself to all-out control of the means of production, thus further illustrating the essentially pragmatic nature of his African-style centralized bureaucracy.

In 1960 the prospects for the survival of the Congo as an entity did not seem great. By 1974 the population had risen to over 20 million spread over nearly one million square miles: it was one of the largest states in the world with very poor communications and national activity exceptionally concentrated in the capital, Kinshasa, which is situated in one corner of the territory. In few countries at this time was the contrast between the services provided by government in cities and rural areas so marked. Only a determined, tough and well-informed politician could survive eight or nine years of power in Zaïre by the necessary manipulation of the different forces to completely subordinate local interests to the authority of the central power. The word 'authority' in this context should, however, not be misinterpreted, for Mobutu had to depend, as much as anything else, on balances of personal and tribal rivalries. Contrary to some critics, he could not afford a prejudice in favour of people from his own province, Equateur. His continuance in office depended at least to some extent on his ability to de-tribalize the public service, which he achieved, as already in-dicated, partly by systematic posting of officials out of their own regions. At the same time, in putting a civilian face on what appeared to be a military régime, President Mobutu found niches in which to represent all the main regional and tribal interests. Such attention to the relative trivia of ad-ministration in its turn concentrated power still further in the President's own office. His blessing or at least tacit agreement was required for each new development at the cost of the per-sonal initiative of officials and a considerable inertia during the periods of Mobutu's increasingly lengthy absences abroad.

In these circumstances, the continuance of the Zaïre régime depends on the extent to which alternative sources of mandate other than the President can emerge. His authority for the expenditure of funds on major projects is required, and since the state commissioners are his nominees the only likely forum for informed debate is the Political Bureau: but here, as within the armed forces, there seems to be a deliberate duality of responsibility arising from the overlapping of areas of activity allocated to different officials and officers. This is a risky pro-cedure viewed in terms other than that of Mobutu's own security and is likely to breed mediocrity and apathy. The rewards of office are, however, correspondingly great, with the national leadership, including the President, apparently deeply involved in development enterprises of all kinds. In no other case in Africa are public office and the paths to personal pros-perity so clearly and openly identified. There is no trace of the appeals for self-denial and austerity superficially characteristic of military and socialist régimes elsewhere.

At the same time the need for national unity at the popular level has not been neglected; in the search for 'authenticity' the systematic name-changing of cities, streets and other topographical features was the essential symbol. People rarely appreciate the extent to which the shambles of 1960–1 in particular, and its news-value abroad, was a matter in the Congo for racial and national shame. The re-creation or indeed initiation of national pride has conventionally required prestige projects – buildings, roads and airlines to which the appropriate labels can be attached. Zaïre has followed this practice and in doing so has inevitably neglected the welfare and standard of living of the people. The question remains for how long popular contentment can be maintained in the face of erratic priorities in which a jumbo jet carrying the Zaïre flag seems to be preferred to any consistent attempt to deal with rocketing food prices. Occasional gestures, inspired perhaps by the Chinese example, towards national unity through the dignity of labour are not likely to be sufficient for long in a country with large reserves of manpower which is still dependent upon mineral revenues earned by foreign companies. The Inga hydro-electric power scheme might well turn out in some senses to be an aid to national unity, but unsatisfied personal expectations expressed in mass unemployment were a serious threat.

In external affairs 1973 was a decisive year for Zaïre. The severance of diplomatic relations with Israel, and the hardening of her attitude towards Southern Africa were in keeping with the new policy towards Peking. Fortuitously, the opportunity provided by the change in America's China policy took the pressure off Mobutu internally, for the withdrawal of Chinese aid to dissidents within Zaïre, and notably in southern Kivu, seemed to be decisive. The decision with regard to Israel was partly to be understood in the context of President Mobutu's bid for African leadership, in which, of course, General Gowon was the principal rival. In this connection he was active in generating consultative meetings between Central African states. However, there were also internal reasons for phasing out Israeli military training assistance which was held not to be entirely suitable for the recruits available as Zaïrean paratroops even though Mobutu himself had for a time trained in Israel. Mobutu's emphasis was from the first on national dignity rather than on submission to some Pan-African authority or concept – hence the conscious attempt to promote and declare a Zaïrean view on international issues. Nevertheless economic commitments to America and Europe, especially Belgium, in spite of the sensitivity of the ex-colonial relationship, are bound to constitute an inhibition when competing with leaders like Gowon, who are free of constraint, or like Haile Selassie, who drew his authority from tradition.

Militarily and in almost all other respects in view of her geographical position, the future of Angola is for Zaïre the most important external question. Mineral interest, communications and contiguity to South-West Africa (Namibia) and, therefore, to South Africa are all important. Zaïrean dependence on Portuguese railways for the export of minerals parallel to some extent the problems experienced by Zambia in developing an independent policy towards Southern Africa.

Mobutu's public declarations about aid to African liberation movements in Angola were almost bound to be at variance with his practical policies. He endeavoured to promote a unification of the MPLA (People's Movement for the Liberation of Angola) and FLNA (National Liberation Front of Angola) but the earlier ideological divide between the two groups remained. The FLNA backed by Zaïre has not been particularly effective: this passivity could be regarded as reflecting Mobutu's recognition of the by no means unique difficulties of his country in acting as a guerilla base.

The general philosophy of the Mobutu government with regard to external relations is easily explicable in terms of the country's internal divisions and their exploitation by the interference of foreign powers since independence in 1960. The question of the secession of Katanga and of collaboration with the industrial strength of the capitalist world contrasted with the promotion of popular rebellion in some provinces, and provided grounds for resentment against both the United States and the Soviet Union. In these conditions non-aligned status was consistent with the economic pragmatism which Mobutu cultivated. There was a strong case for a kind of isolationist independence which the size of the country and Mobutu's style of government seemed in any case to promote.

The government of the Congo (Zaïre) since 1965 has been in almost all respects more personal than military. President Mobutu Sese Seko was described at the time of his state visit to London variously as 'A Henry Tudor after the Wars of the Roses, or a Richelieu after the Wars of Religion' or, more tentatively, as a General Lyautey bringing law and order where there had been chaos and anarchy.* Whatever the true nature of the régime, he used the military and civilian apparatus to restore unity and to eliminate overt rebellion; he allowed the rise of an African bourgeoisie within an essentially capitalist framework and at the same time cultivated the university and its products. He kept his authority by cutting out his rivals and was at the same time apparently not insensitive to their fate. Not being in the mainstream of African nationalism he only occasionally sought ideological justification for his actions. In many ways his most remarkable achievement has been to survive his past association of military service with journalism and political activity in Patrice Lumumba's *Mouvement Nationale Congolaise* (MNC) which was the feature of his career up to 1960 when he brought about his first coup. His régime since 1965 can be said to have thrown more light on the problems of political control in a large African state than on the political behaviour of the military, whom Mobutu has tended to treat as only one of several elements in the balance of forces in Zaïre which he has sought to achieve.

* In *West Africa*, No. 2948, 10 December 1973, 1717.

VII · General Amin's Uganda

It could be argued that, in terms of the political influence of a single man, there is a direct comparison to be made between Mobutu's Zaïre and Amin's Uganda. Both men were once sergeants in colonial armies and both had asserted their leadership in a period of mutiny and general military discontent; in some senses their approach to nationalism in its economic form was parallel. But while Mobutu, though still something of an enigma, invited calm, dispassionate appraisal of his achievements, Amin excited violent emotions and reactions, as well as speculations about his state of health. Many well-substantiated reports of killings in Makindiye Military Prison, Kampala, reached the international press, and it seemed certain that respected citizens like the Chief Justice, Benedicto Kiwanuka and the Vice-Chancellor of the University, Frank Kalamuzo, had disappeared.

A range of questions require answers. Was Amin's seizure of power a military coup in the ordinary sense? Were his own motives other than strictly personal? To what extent did he represent a continuation of or break with the mainstream of Ugandan politics since independence? What was the rationale, if any, of the policies pursued, particularly in relation to an assertion of economic nationalism? Any explanation must go some way to reconciling an astonishing range of public declarations and actions ranging from the ruthless and rapid expulsion of the Asians, to Amin's approval, in the context of modern Israel, of Hitler's treatment of the Jews and weird gestures of good intention, such as starting a fund with £600 to aid Britain in her economic difficulties.

Amin's 'unique' personality was at first widely accepted

as a convenient explanation for all the developments in modern Uganda. The accuracy of this proposition may yet be confirmed, but as a hypothesis it needs to be tested against the degree of acceptance and popularity which Amin's policies have achieved in some quarters in and outside Uganda. His expulsion of the Asians in the cause of establishing an African Uganda struck a chord in Kenya to the embarrassment of that country's government; similarly, his action against foreign commercial interests and the expulsion of the Israeli military assistance team was enthusiastically supported by his own people. It could well be argued that in terms of power within Uganda he did no more than his predecessor, Milton Obote, had done in basing his authority on his strength in his own region and tribe. Thus in the army and elsewhere the Langi and Acholi men favoured by Obote were replaced by Kakwa, Amin's own tribe, Lugbara and Madi. He was not even responsible for the initiation as a primary element in politics of the army, or factions within it, though his eventual personal manipulation of it had been on the cards since his intervention at the time of the mutiny in 1964. The politicization of the army dated back to that event and to Obote's use of it to dispose of Baganda influence. It could be that Amin's régime, though it weakened Uganda's economic prospects, will prove to be another monument to the political effectiveness of devious and almost whimsical patronage combined with the habitual use of force, of which there are many historical examples.

The mutiny of 1964 began the process of politicizing the army and at the same time established the position of Idi Amin within it. The Ugandan army at independence suffered from a grave dearth of African officers: there were none with any substantial commissioned experience. This was partly the result of Bagandan reluctance to join. Between independence in 1961 and the mutiny in 1964 the situation had deteriorated. On the one hand, the relationship of the central government under Obote with the kingdom of Baganda emerged as the principal political issue; on the other, race relations between British expatriate officers and young Ugandans within the army quickly became extremely sensitive. The direct intervention of ministers and their overt sympathy for the soldiers' grievances led to the opening of political channels for complaints by African subordinates against their white superiors. Ministers were tempted to curry popularity by listening to grievances in such a way as to encourage indiscipline. Poor accommodation, lack of promotion and, because of the neighbouring Congo and Sudan situations, an awareness of political potentialities combined to stir up trouble. The spark which led to the explosion, however, came across the border from Tanganyika, where in January 1964 the army mutinied at Colito Barracks outside Dar-es-Salaam for improvements in pay and conditions and more rapid replacement of British expatriates. Before British troops from Kenya could be invited to intervene, a massive pay rise, agreed to by a minister virtually under duress, had been announced. It was the intervention of Major Amin at this stage which achieved confirmation by the Prime Minister of the pay rise as well as the promise of Africanization of key posts. Amin at once assumed the appointment of Commanding Officer of the battalion at Jinja barracks. The mutiny typically left scars and thereafter rumours of conspiracies were endemic, centering round the rival personalities of the two senior officers, Major-General Amin and Brigadier Opolot.

The next important event was the army's overwhelmingly violent assault on the Kabaka of Buganda's palace in February 1966. Idi Amin, as Field Commander of the army, helped to pave the way for a republic and for Milton Obote's presidency involving a so-called 'Move to the Left'. The representation of the clash between Obote and the Kabaka as one between progress and the *status quo* was convenient if misleading. In seeking to broaden the base of his support Obote emphasized the class basis of the struggle and grew increasingly suspicious of rivals – an attitude which was to say the least exacerbated by the assassination attempt of December 1969. Thereafter, Major-General Amin and other close associates were suspect. Like Nkrumah before him, Obote developed a special quasi-military force and, under Akena Adoko, a new version of the police General Service Unit which was in effect a secret police. This, combined with preferential promotion of Langi and Acholi officers, threatened the status and safety of men like Amin. They in their turn had their allies in the Cabinet including Felix Onama, the Minister of Defence, who had negotiated with the soldiers in 1964. The entrenchment of Langi and Acholi influence was the key factor in promoting militant hostility to Obote in that his version of socialism was also seen as undermining those existing economic interests which preferred the benefits of free enterprise.

1964 had taught the army the effectiveness of the violent threat which it could wield against the government. Discipline had been weakened by the retention of mutinous soldiers. The campaign against the Baganda subsequently adjusted them to the intimidation of sectors of the population. Obote's attempts to cultivate the army were necessarily indiscriminate in the distribution of extra pay and allowances, but he had relied unduly on the consequences of Langi and Acholi promotions. In apparently identifying Amin as the most important potential focus for opposition within the army the President showed some perception. His departure for Singapore clearly involved considerable risk at a time when, as seen in retrospect, confrontation had become inevitable. In the event Amin, with the support of part of the army including the vital mechanized elements, was to win the struggle for survival. The plausibility of the view that Amin's action was a pre-emptive strike which incidentally became a coup and gave him power is obvious. It is not, however, the only possible explanation and at least requires some qualification.

In the first place, it is unlikely that Obote would have left the country at that time had the crisis seemed inevitable or the tension more than usually acute. The conditions of corruption, tribal rivalries, criminal activity and alienation between government and military command had existed for some time. Nor was the army, largely because of his treatment of it, a united body or one in which the ranks were likely to close because of a perceived threat to its integrity from his quarter. Indeed it is probable that Obote, in insisting before his departure for Singapore that Amin should account for financial and other malpractices within the army, was actually relying on its fragmentation. The most likely explanation is that both Obote, in remaining in Singapore slightly too long after hearing news of unrest in Uganda, and Amin, in reacting to rumours of an intention to depose him, precipitated the crisis. Amin's mobilization of the armoured troops to back him drew from Obote public antagonism which led Amin to consolidate his seizure of power for his own personal safety. Thereafter Amin was in the position of winning a brief civil war in which the army was as divided as the nation, and becoming entrenched as a result of a realignment of Uganda's tribal factions into a new pattern. There seemed to be no deliberately planned coup and there was certainly no programme of policies or any real motivation. One ruling group had been overthrown by another in an atmosphere of alleged conspiracy and counter-conspiracy, muddle and personal opportunism.

The Uganda affair of 25 January 1971 was evidently not the natural or inevitable culmination of previous events involving the spasmodic but progressive convergence of general and military discontent. Though like other military intrusions into politics in Africa, the so-called Amin coup took place in unique local circumstances, it did provide some grounds for questioning the validity of accepted interpretations of earlier events elsewhere. Chance and opportunism are clearly likely to be underrated by political analysts anxious to discern a pattern or to construct a model. In the case of Uganda events have shown that the interpretation of the coup itself is vital to an understanding of the régime which followed.

Amin's followers went through all the usual motions of self-justification and presenting themselves to the populace as heroes. It was not difficult to proclaim the evils of corruption, of imprisonment without trial, of financial misappropriation, of secret police activities and of tribally divisive actions. There were many people who could at least temporarily rejoice on being relieved of the repression of the Obote administration. Quite apart from Amin's own personal power base, tribal and military, the ex-President had created at different times enough enemies to rally to the alternative champion. Steps were quickly taken to eliminate Langi and Acholi dominance in the army. This was achieved not only by recruiting Kakwa and Lugbara, but by enlisting what were in effect mercenary troops, Southern Sudanese refugees from their own civil war and soldiers who were alleged to be Congolese, possibly the remnants of Mulele's rebels. Long before the abortive 'counter-coup' of March 1974, Amin's reliance on a 'power base' in the West Nile Province and on Nubian soldiers from inside and outside Uganda had begun to turn sour on him. He had to purge senior Lugbara elements from the army because of signs of unrest and it was clearly more significant that Brigadier Charles Arrube, who 'died' in the clash on 24 March 1974, was a Christian from Amin's own tribe the Kakwa, than that he had been training for a year in Russia. There was also the resentment of the people of Baganda to be cultivated, who, deprived by Obote not only of their Kabaka but of what they felt to be their proper rewards, were ready to support Amin. Not all prominent Obote men were excluded from office: some were clearly useful in countering factionalism. The ruthless selectivity shown in choosing who should serve the new régime, and who should be eliminated or driven into exile, was a notable feature of the administration.

Contrary to some reports General Amin did not neglect the

possibilities, often demonstrated by colonial rulers, of enlisting the assistance of the necessary number of local collaborators to make domination by another tribe or tribes acceptable. Like Obote before him, and the more astute African leaders elsewhere, Amin seemed to appreciate the need for diversity of tribal support in order to secure country-wide control. Under him, however, the Ugandan position on the southern frontier of Islam in Africa acquired a new importance. Whereas previously the Catholic–Protestant split had been an important feature of Uganda politics, now Moslems, though small in number, were favoured in the army and in commerce and gradually the President identified himself with militant Islam in North Africa and the Middle East. It was natural that he should be drawn into communion with Colonel Qaddafi in Libya. If the disappearance of a number of prominent Catholics like Kiwanuka was more than a coincidence, then a new politics–religious opposition alignment would become a possibility in Uganda, namely a Catholic–Protestant alliance.

Unlike, for example, the military governments of Nigeria and Ghana, the Amin administration acted to reduce the influence not only of politicians but of civil servants. In February 1973 Cabinet ministers were given one month's leave pending retirement for the whole Cabinet; this was no doubt due to the fact that most of the ministers were non-military. If Amin relied on any continuous advice at all it was that of the relatively senior officers in the Defence Council, but there were some who said not altogether facetiously that he countenanced only divine guidance! After three years of the new style of administration – a not wholly appropriate term – no ideological or conventional rationale of government was yet discernible, the only criterion being individual or group self-interest. The interpretative question was how to reconcile the expulsion of the Ugandan Asians, the reduction of foreign commercial interests and the more or less consequent economic decline, the elimination of prominent critics and the provocation of hostilities with Tanzania, as well as the expansion of the army at great expense in equipment to around 20,000 men.

If one simply assumes that this illustrates a dictatorship by an erratic personality then perhaps no further explanation would be needed. It is, however, more likely that all this is the expression of a new form of the kind of sub-nationalism which Obote himself had created. On this basis, which might be vulgarly described as that of 'winner-takes-all', each successive ruler is entitled to appropriate to his own élite group not only all power, but all the profits to be obtained from its exercise. Hence the allocation of the better Asian businesses apparently to Muslim Africans and the elevation, especially within the expanded armed forces, of Amin's fellow tribesmen and their supporters; hence also the need to ensure the silencing of any opposition, however practically ineffective. In circumstances where power is everything it could be argued that the general prosperity of the country is not important, only the sharing of what wealth there is amongst those who matter. This, it might be claimed, was simply what had prevailed before in post-independence Uganda accentuated and rendered more brutal by the 'invasion' of 1972, and by the guerilla threat imposed from exile by the previous régime. Uganda seems to be in the care of a régime for which there are no conventional rules and from which the pretence of concern for the good of the people at large has been stripped. If this is true there is nothing here of the legend of the military as 'the knights in shining armour' defending the honour and reputation of the state, except in the crudest terms.

A charitable view of the situation in Uganda might be to claim that at independence forces were unleashed which established an ultimately competitive style of politics. Amin's personal conduct in relation to the Ugandan peoples, and sometimes even to others, often had an air of naïvely paternal simplicity patently derived from what can only be termed his religious and military faiths, both essentially authoritarian.

Though not conforming to any of the usual modes of military régime, that in Uganda within a short period of its inception had installed force as the unique basis of Uganda politics. The dynamic escalation of violence followed to the point where the President evidently realized the threat which its indiscriminate use posed to him and to the state by alienating large segments of the population. The evident advantages of positive economic nationalism which could have derived from a more gradual expulsion of the Ugandan Asians had not been used to unify the country behind its military leader.

VIII · The Military in the Sudan

It is often forgotten that of all the modern independent African states the military have had a longer experience in the Sudan than anywhere else except Egypt. In a sense this could be attributed to the facts that not only had the British administration of the territory been of an essentially military character but the Sudan Defence Force and a military college to go with it had been established at a very early stage. In strict terms 'localization' of the officer corps of this force began in 1918 even before such a development had been seriously contemplated in India. All this, of course, related to the crucial strategic position of the Sudan, lying as it does between the nascent nationalism of Egypt and the ancient kingdom of Ethiopia. The maturity of the Sudanese military was confirmed by the rôle they played in the recovery of Ethiopia from Italian domination in the Second World War. It is, however, worth recalling that in 1924 Sudanese army units mutinied, and armed cadets from the military school demonstrated, against the withdrawal of Egyptian troops from the Sudan. Abdallah Khalil, who subsequently in the rôle of Prime Minister played the leading part in initiating the 1958 coup, was then a young officer and a member of the nationalist White Flag League. It was an event eventually more significant for relations with Egypt than with Britain.

The pioneering 1958 coup in the Sudan conformed more or less to the classic model of military political opportunism in that the changes which were effected were more of personnel than policies; the prime difference lay in the source of the initiative. The four-year-old Sudanese government was struggling in a deteriorating economic situation to cope with a run on the foreign exchange reserves, with industrial strikes which were wrecking new enterprises and with an apparently unmanageable rebellion in the Southern Sudan. A weak coalition government dependent on volatile parliamentary support was patently not the best instrument to reassure a sensitive people against the rumoured possibility of an Egyptian take-over by whatever means. The disillusionment of the educated élite with the manoeuvrings of inexperienced politicians was almost total and certainly sufficient to justify the confidence of Major-General Ibrahim Abboud in responding to the request of his contemporary and school friend the Prime Minister that he should take power temporarily. He was, however, reluctant to take this drastic step and in spite of the example of Nasser in neighbouring Egypt was clearly unprepared practically and ideologically. The first phase of military rule in the Sudan – the years 1958–64 – reflected this unpreparedness. Not uniquely, the re-establishment of economic and political stability followed by an unobtrusive return to barracks proved easier to imagine than to achieve.

The foundations of military rule, as with its civil predecessor, had been built on the morass of inter-relationships and rivalries between political parties and religious sects which was characteristic of the Sudan. The volatility of the political alignments was primarily due to the deep divisions between the Khatmiyya and the Ansar which had inevitably grown worse under British control. For these were not only religious but increasingly socio-economic groups and urbanization and the expansion of trade was bound to affect their relations. The Khatmiyya, being based primarily in the North of the country along the Nile, included those who had seized the opportunity to become traders, whereas the Ansar were closely identified with traditional authority, large family estates and peasant subsistence agriculture. The Umma party became associated with Ansar (Mahdist) interests, while the Khatmiyya supported one of the continually changing alternatives. The military junta – in the form of the Supreme Council of the Armed Forces under the presidency of General Ibrahim Abboud – had not only to manage this complex situation but also to respond to the demands of militant trades unions and in due course also of a radical Free Officer Organization which drew its support from the socially new style officers recruited in 1953. The farmers of the Gezira cotton scheme were strongly placed to apply pressures to a government which showed signs of weakness. The coup temporarily and nominally resolved the inter-party bickering, and allowed the new régime a breathing space to make some progress with the economic crisis at a time when the cost of living and a controversy over the acceptance of American aid had provoked trades union demonstrations.

The setting up of a military government enabled the banning not only of political parties but also of strikes and demonstrations. By accepting a realistic cotton price accumulated surpluses were quickly disposed of and the sterling reserves rose in nine months from £4·8 million to about £30 million and in the following year doubled again. This dramatic change in the balance of trade coupled with budgetary caution encouraged foreign investment and assistance. The arrangements under the Nile Waters Agreement for water for irrigation assisted the development of a number of the new projects which were soon underway. Land reform, housing schemes and profits from the cash sales of crops quickly improved the lot of the average Sudanese in the northern part of the country.

But economic success, for it clearly was such, was not enough to offset the political inexperience and ineptitude of the administration. Not only was it tempted to embark on the kind of vast and ambitious enterprises which were particularly fertile in opportunities for corruption and misappropriation, but in a curious way there was an almost complete failure to acquire popular credit for the initial economic improvements. The estrangement between military government and people thereafter followed a familiar course. Alienation arising from a sense of remoteness of the leaders was reinforced by their own increased enjoyment of the privileges and trappings of power. Reluctance to assume responsibility gave way to neglect of civilian advice and an apparent unawareness of the need to cultivate a popular consensus.

In this situation the fissures which had appeared in the army hierarchy at a very early stage assumed an increasing importance. Some senior officers felt that their exclusion from office was due to their not being Umma party supporters. Indeed the army's divisions corresponded to those in the country at large and there seem to have been at least three attempted coups within the officer structure. The large number of younger officers appointed from 1953 onwards generally sympathized with the more radical political elements against both the established politicians and their own leadership. The eventual escalation of the war in the south, which accentuated economic difficulties by draining resources and nullified the previous gains, reduced the administration to a state of near collapse.

In a situation in which expulsions and dismissals had shifted the carefully established balance of sectarian and party interests within the Supreme Military Council, charges by the military rank and file of incompetence in the field were difficult to withstand. While predictably instituting repressive measures which at first forced organized opposition underground, the Military Council admitted the existence of a stalemate on the Southern Sudan question by appointing a commission of enquiry and inviting public discussion. This unleashed a demand by students for a political rather than a military solution to the problem, which quickly gathered momentum and was converted into a general revolt. The movement for the return of civilian rule even had the support of the younger, more radical element in the officer corps, and of civil servants who practised their own form of civil disobedience by obstructing the bureaucratic processes by delay in carrying out instructions. A general strike in the Khartoum area led to demonstrations by dissident groups drawn from almost all sectors of the community, including judges, magistrates, university lecturers, trades unionists and Gezira farmers. The popular sympathies of the junior officers split the army and the military régime had little alternative but to dissolve itself when it was surrounded by elements of the armed forces as it consulted in the palace.

A number of factors had contributed to the Supreme Council's fall from the pedestal on which it had placed itself after 1958. Army factions had overtly competed for power. There had been too much concentration of administrative detail in the hands of the Council and petty decisions about scholarships and attendance at conferences had attracted odium which might well have been left to the civil service. The uprooting of some 50,000 Nubians of Wadi Halfa to make way for the consequences of the Aswan High Dam had been badly handled in circumstances in which the educated element knew that the Sudan had done badly in its own terms for compensation out of the Nile Waters Agreement of 1959. At the same time the students of Khartoum University were not by any means for the last time disaffected. Clandestine political opposition flourished on the campus. Some felt that university autonomy and authoritarian rule were demonstrably incompatible – an understandable view.

There were typically clashes between military governors and civil servants over demarcation of responsibilities. At the same time the trades union movement was angry at government interference. Finally, an abrupt change of direction on the problem of the Southern Sudan and ill-prepared consultation with civilian bodies had unleashed outpourings of criticism.

The Sudanese October Revolution of 1964 was unusual in that the convergence of military with professional and intellectual unrest led to the establishment of a civilian government reflecting the original political parties, who in the event were within three months unable to agree on the weighting of

electoral representation as between town and country. The
Free Officer Movement had withdrawn from the scene, only
to re-emerge in 1969. The coup of May 1969 was in no real sense
a repetition of that of 1958; rather it was the establishment in
power of those forces within the army which had contributed
to the overthrow of the military régime in 1964. This time it
was clearly appreciated that a reformed army would have to
play an overt role in supporting a new administration.

The then Colonel Jaafer-al-Nimeiry became head of a
National Revolutionary Council which consisted with one exception, the former chief justice, of young army officers. The
old political parties were in effect displaced by independent
radicals, some with Marxist sympathies. It was made clear at
an early stage by the military Minister of the Interior that the
support of Communists in an effort to transform society would
not be rejected. At first Nimeiry blamed the heavy national
debts and generally depressed economic situation on colonialism and proclaimed his intentions of expanding trade relations
with Arab and Communist countries and of replacing foreign
capital by the development of public sector enterprises. A
socialist trend internally was to be combined with non-align-
ment externally. Nimeiry had long associations with political
activity in the army having twice, in 1957 and 1966, been detained for this reason. He organized popular demonstrations in
favour of the Revolutionary Council and purged by retirement
the senior elements of the army and the police force. Pains were
taken to consolidate the security position of the régime by the
publication of a soldiers' charter.

The unity of the army, the solution of the Southern problem
and the resuscitation of the ailing economy were the main tasks
to be faced, and in association with these the setting in train of
some kind of programme of social reform. The Revolutionary
Council announced its recognition of the right of the Southern
provinces to regional autonomy within a united Sudan.
The defeat of the Ansar rising led to a redistribution of the

large estates among the peasants and in May 1970, as a step not only towards economic independence but to breaking up some of the other traditional vested interests, the nationalization of banks and foreign commercial firms was announced. Nimeiry was beginning effectively to identify the political forces of the left with a reformed and reforming military. The desirability and possibility of using the military as an agent of social change was, however, quickly a matter for debate. The example of the Free Officers' Movement in Egypt in seizing power was attractive, but the question was whether there, as elsewhere, the army had in fact consolidated a system based on a lower middle class which would in its turn obstruct a popular revolution.

After 1970 the Nimeiry régime seemed to become gradually less concerned with ideology and more pragmatic in its approach to both external and internal problems. The President was applauded by the Communist powers, with whom he quickly established special relationships, and also by the militant Arabs including Colonel Qaddafi of Libya. The Sudan's association with the British faded, largely due to nationalization and the ensuing argument over compensation to British interests, and diplomatic relations were actually severed with the United States and West Germany, as a result of Sudan's support of the Arabs during the Six Day War. The new alignment, however, did not solve the country's economic problems. Soviet aid proved unsatisfactory and the Chinese, though conscientious and thorough in what they provided, were not involved on a large scale. There was in any case within the ruling council an unsuspectedly severe ideological division in spite of the declared revolutionary objective.

In one sense a turning point came in July 1971 with a conspiracy between certain elements in the army officer corps and the proscribed Communist party to overthrow Nimeiry. The loyalty of the main body of the armed forces procured his rescue and reinstatement, but uncharacteristically the Soviet

Union had openly backed the venture and relations between Khartoum and Moscow broke down.

In the meantime the Addis Ababa Agreement had brought an end to the bloody civil war in the Southern Sudan at the price of diluting Arab and Islamic influences in the government. This ruled out any immediate possibility of Sudanese association with an Egypt–Libya federation as was then being promoted by Qaddafi. Nimeiry's achievement not only in bringing the conflict to an end but in carrying out far-reaching measures of reconciliation is akin to that of Gowon in Nigeria after the civil war there. Within a year, for example, Major-General Joseph Lager, albeit Israeli-trained, had been converted from an 'Anyanya' rebel into Inspector-General of the Army of the Sudan and a confidant of the President. More than a million ordinary people had returned from displacement in the bush or foreign exile to resume their normal lives. With the aid of international agencies comprehensive resettlement had taken place in a forbidding part of the world. An autonomous Southern Region government at Juba was integrated into the federal government and elections had been held. It is questionable whether anyone other than a military leader with the political views of General Nimeiry could not only have created confidence in place of raw, violent antagonism but actually absorbed many of the rebels into the army, police and prison services.

The unity of the Sudan consequently seems to depend on his survival in office. He has naturally not been without bitter opposition. The resistance to Nimeiry's Southern policy of conciliation came to a head in an Arab Socialist conspiracy. These elements were quickly and quietly removed from government, but while Nimeiry endeavoured to mobilize the country as a one-party state under the banner of the Sudan Socialist Union, they continued to plot against him from Tripoli and Cairo. The killing of Western diplomats, two Americans and a Belgian, in Khartoum, was evidently the work of

Black September Palestinians; Nimeiry dealt firmly with this attempt to embarrass his adjusted foreign policy and brought those allegedly responsible to trial.

Internally Nimeiry, though a Muslim himself, had to resist pressures from the Muslim Brothers aimed at upsetting the conciliation of the non-Muslim South and at establishing a puritanical Islamic Republic which would certainly not be popular with the sophisticated Khartoum élite. In the process Nimeiry apparently came to understand the need for diversity of external support and aid, and perhaps appreciated that he was less at risk from former 'imperialists' than from new-found 'friends', especially if his prime aim was economic recovery. The restoration of diplomatic links with Bonn and Washington and a five-day state visit to London in March 1973 were signs of mutual recognition of the merits of his style of pragmatic independence. He nevertheless remained committed to his own concept of revolutionary socialism and his stance on the Palestinian question continued firm.

As President in a military régime General Nimeiry had in his first four years managed to achieve acceptance of his solution of the grave problem of the South and was feeling his way towards economic independence for the Sudan, for him a most sensitive topic. Like other military leaders before him, he had felt it necessary to order the execution of the Communists who sought to overthrow him in July 1971. In the Sudan over fifteen or so years a conventional, *ad hoc* conservative military régime was replaced by one with at least the semblance of an ideologically distinctive policy, which sought its own definition of the national interest within the framework of a complex world and Middle Eastern situation.

IX · Conclusions

The seizure of power is one thing and the constructive exercise of it quite another. This is the first inevitable, if rather obvious conclusion to be reached from an examination of current or recent military régimes in Africa. The conduct of the military in government generally reflects the spontaneous and initially haphazard character of most *coups d'état*. Not only is a defined ideology or considered political programme a rare feature amongst African military élites before intervention in politics, but they do not usually even seek to justify on a doctrinaire or philosophical basis the régimes which they establish. Pragmatism prevails and is quickly restored even when, as with General Nimeiry of the Sudan, there was a hint of something more systematic to begin with.

The prevalence in Africa, as also in Latin America, of military rule or of political change inspired, promoted or made possible by the military, is of itself good ground for caution in making sweeping analytic generalizations. The countries concerned and the governments established have been themselves so diverse as to make worthwhile an investigation of the hypothesis that there is little to choose between military régimes, which are in any case often half-civilian in composition, and civilian régimes, which inevitably rely on the support of the army for their continuance in power. In one form or another armies have played a direct political rôle at some time in at least thirty out of forty African states since independence.

The admittedly widespread influence of the British, French and other European military traditions has suggested, particularly to those who for their own purposes wished to believe it, that the epidemic of military coups was fomented by Western agents wishing to assert neo-colonialist influence in Africa. If the CIA, MI5 or the French Secret Service were not directly responsible, then it would at least be very convenient for the powers concerned to enjoy vicarious power through their 'stooges' trained in their military schools. Objectively, however, it is hard to deny that many military leaders of Africa have behaved in power with a marked degree of independence which could in some cases be termed erratic and totally unpredictable. In Congo-Brazzaville, for example, President Ngouabi, a professed Marxist, conducted his government accordingly; on the other hand, his near neighbour Bokassa of the Central African Republic had no recognizable ideology and at the same time belied the cultivated image for which any French mentors would have wished. There is little in common between the governments established in the Somali Republic and Libya: one is heavily involved with international socialism of both the Russian and Chinese varieties while the other, which is militantly Islamic in character, having overthrown a feudal monarchy categorically rejects communism and buys weapon systems from France.

The six main cases discussed in this book are sufficiently varied to confirm this impression. Even the contrast between the first and second military régimes in Ghana is enough to bring firmly into question the view, not unnaturally expressed by Kwame Nkrumah after his deposition in 1966, that the officers concerned were more attached to British customs and tradition than to the Ghanaian way of life. Neither General Gowon of Nigeria nor General Amin in Uganda, in their very different ways, can be justifiably condemned as lackeys of the British. While in Dahomey the army leaders have been largely concerned to balance the complex political interests in order to provide spasmodic stability, Generals Mobutu of Zaïre and Nimeiry of the Sudan have apparently tried to develop their own characteristic forms of economic nationalism. Afrifa in Ghana organized an early return to civilian rule, Gowon in

Nigeria envisaged some move in that direction by 1976, while Mobutu in Zaïre presides over an essentially civilianized government where the army is treated as one among a set of interests on whose interaction his power depends.

In varying degrees all these military régimes have turned to civil servants and other civilian experts not only to help them administer the country but for the formulation of policy. They have suspended political parties, though there has, as in Zaïre, been some tendency to create a new quasi-political nexus of associations under another label with the head of state as its centre. The tendencies of the first generation of African politicians to generate nationally destructive strife has been curbed, but at the same time the military–civil service alliances have not been notably productive of innovation. The routine administration of the military has combined with the fear of the civilian for his neck or his job to prevent the instigation of radical change. The army's claim to be able to control corruption has been constantly made but only spasmodically upheld; the likelihood is that the umbrella of the military will by its very nature encourage the quiet, undercover resolution of administrative difficulties in order to keep the wheels of the machine turning apparently smoothly. Similarly, a false sense of national unity and security has been created by the vision of a uniformed leader presenting himself to cheering crowds as saviour or restorer of the country's honour. The cases of Dahomey recurrently, and of the Sudan in 1964 and 1969, demonstrate clearly the inherent risk of repeated coups once the unconstitutional method becomes a substitute for constitutional procedures. But, it may well be asked, what other techniques for achieving a change of government have been effectively demonstrated in the African context? The question remains whether there are any features of the political–social–economic development of relevant African countries which can be directly attributed to the existence of military régimes.

It is not sufficient to say that active military intervention is only an episode in the continuous stream of civil–military relations, whether the army is in or out of power. Some of the assumptions already made more or less consciously in this book clearly require testing – for example, the general belief, deriving from a stereotyped view of the operation of military organizations, that army officers are good at routine administration but cannot govern. This involves a comparison with absolute or at least external standards: if internal comparisons are made as between, for example, the economic policies of Acheampong on the one hand, and either Nkrumah or Busia on the other, then the superiority in this respect of the current military government might well be asserted. Such a conclusion might, however, relate to the extent to which the civil servants in that administration have a freer hand than before. Dr Busia's expulsion of aliens in order to alleviate unemployment without considering the effect on the economy might well be set beside General Amin's treatment of the Asians in Uganda. The point is simply that any worthwhile assessment of the performance of the military in government in Africa must be made in terms of the alternative political talent available and not of an external reference group or set of alien norms. Such qualities as the ability to conciliate diverse factions within the state or to mobilize a consensus of support within the country are on the evidence available as likely or unlikely to be possessed by military as by civilian governments. The question remains to what extent military government is a distinctive form of government in the spectrum of administrations prevailing in developing countries.

In considering the incidence of coups emphasis has often been placed on the extent to which the army officer's background differs institutionally from that of his civilian counterpart. This has led to an evident underestimate of the similarities in social background to which the success, and relative bloodlessness of some military coups, has been incidentally attributed. The evidence from Ghana, for example, suggests that the emphasis should be on the similarities rather than the dissimilarities. In spite of their long specialized training, sometimes in part outside the country, soldier and civilian officials have tended to come from comparable social backgrounds, to go to the same schools, to maintain contact in their leisure time, and inevitably to be related, if only by marriage. The small size of the officer corps has made it unlikely that the degree of isolation found in some European military circles would survive. Just as an African officer corps often has an external reference group in the shape of the European military élite to whom it owes its training and essential professional attitudes, so may the civil servants in the same country have derived their values from their opposite numbers in Britain or France or from former colonial administrators nurtured in the same tradition. The claim that the military have a different socio-economic interest from their civilian counterparts is blurred by these factors as well as by the consideration that, in any case, the government of the day holds the key to financial gain and economic progress for all groups. A kind of 'spoils' system may exist which is found only exceptionally in Western democracies. It is indeed apparent that only where a threat has been shown to exist to the security and identity of the military establishment separately from that of the civilian establishment does any real dichotomy occur.

It cannot be denied, however, that some problems arise in government which are the direct product of the military nature of the administration. The techniques involved in establishing legitimacy after a violent change of government clearly come into this category, though as changes of government by due electoral or other constitutional process are rare in Africa the problem is not one which only the military experience. All the military régimes so far discussed display evidence of some tensions arising from this cause; ready substitutes for the popular communication channels associated with the mass political party are by no means obvious. In some cases they first take the form of a symbolic policy, for example, 'One Nigeria', or the expropriation or limitation of foreign interests as in Colonel Acheampong's Ghana or more drastically in Uganda. Only the cultivation of consensus or the possession of thoroughly reliable instruments of coercion can establish a government for long enough for it to be regarded as the rightful authority.

Ideally, the evident success of the government in improving the condition of the people should be sufficient to establish it, but in the circumstances prevailing in Africa this is rarely achievable. Ironically, the rise in world cocoa prices in 1972–3 probably did more to establish the legitimacy of the Acheampong government in Ghana than any of the deliberate measures taken. General Gowon's ability to enhance Nigerian prestige externally, while conciliating the ex-Biafrans, has served him well; so, to all appearances, has General Nimeiry's handling of the problem of the South Sudan, in spite of the consequent anger of the more militant Pan-Arabists, worked in his favour. Sometimes the search for or cultivation of civilian allies proves a source of weakness rather than of strength, but the suggestion that the writ of the central government runs throughout the country, as in Nigeria and the Sudan, is as effective as anything. It is indeed difficult to disassociate the re-establishment of legitimacy from the ability of the government to demonstrate its might, though that in its turn may prove counter-productive.

While the maintenance of channels of communication with the people remains an obvious problem, it is possible that in the African political context the reconciliation of conflicting interests can be better achieved by a national army, if that it is. However, the supposedly temporary nature of military rule poses the additional problem of ensuring the future security in all senses of members of the government and their close supporters. A large army like that of Nigeria which might, on economic grounds, be required by a civilian administration to stage a rapid demobilization to a fraction of its existing size clearly constitutes an especial difficulty. Nevertheless the basic problems in African countries vary not so much with the style of the régime as with the general state of their situation. Where economic viability, national unity and security, external and internal, are as in most cases the main concerns the differences in behaviour between military and civilian governments are necessarily limited. Indeed elusive economic viability is likely to produce or be associated with conditions conducive to a low level of political culture where recurrent changes of government are likely. In a country like Dahomey the resistance of the population to the initiation of military rule is clearly minimal: in these conditions the changes in style of government are not likely to be, indeed cannot be, great. The institutions and procedures remain essentially the same, only the groupings of interests and, therefore, the disposition of patronage are likely to change, though, as already reiterated, under a military régime spontaneous contacts between government and governed may be more difficult.

In short, coups are demonstrably most likely to occur in countries where the political system is immature, national unity is fragile and economic progress is difficult if not impossible: these are generally the same countries where the similarity in background and interests of soldier and civilian is likely to be greatest. It is therefore not surprising that, on the one hand, the style of government depends more on the character of the head of state, as with Amin or Mobutu, than on the fact that he is soldier or civilian, and that, on the other hand, the greater differences are likely to be apparent where the maturity of civil and military institutions is more advanced, as in Ghana or Nigeria.

The fact that any state, however small and backward, is a more complex organism than an army means that military leaders in political rôles depend on finding other interest groups to support them. These will not necessarily be the same groups as politicians will cultivate. Their professional outlook

and training may predispose them to alliance with the civil
service as the group closest in experience and background to
their own, though there were signs of strain in Afrifa's Ghana
as to some extent in Gowon's Nigeria due to misconceptions
about the function of bureaucracy. Nevertheless they are
likely, as in Ghana, to share an anti-political attitude: indeed
as Nkrumah's stock declined there were in the early 1960s
observers who predicted that a coup would be initiated in the
higher echelons of the civil service. Correspondingly, chiefs or
traditional leaders are likely to prove more natural allies for
the military than trades union and youth leaders. Where the
latter have emerged within a military framework, as in the
Congo Republic, the régime has inclined to a more radical
ideology. In Africa so far the armed forces have been too small
and poorly established to allow for the emergence of a régime
in which the military could effectively stand alone. Generally
they have followed their civilian predecessors in relying on the
bureaucracy and developed socio-economic interests: the
political party had often itself proved an unreliable instrument
in the African one-party state.

It may, however, be argued that it is not the style of a
government which matters but the policies it pursues: in other
words, the message is more important than the medium. To
what extent have military rulers in fact pursued distinctive
policies? Have they proved more or less 'radical' than their
civilian counterparts? Judged from the standpoint of domestic
policies it is very hard to generalize. In the ideological sense
General Amin would be regarded by many as more conservative than General Gowon, but he has adopted a more strongly
nationalist policy in dealing with foreign commercial interests.
In this respect the distinction between Colonel Acheampong,
and Dr Nkrumah three governments before him, is not really
clear, except that the current head of state in Ghana seems to
temper any ideology with pragmatism to the point that his
policies seem to make the more consistent sense to the outside

observer. The proper conclusion, reviewing the activities of Generals Mobutu, Gowon, Nimeiry and Colonel Acheampong, is perhaps that military governments are less prone to ideological commitment and more likely to take a pragmatic and opportunist view of the national interest. This would be consistent with the reasonably well validated axiom that such régimes are better at day-to-day administration than at the formulation of policies. It would tend to coincide with Zolberg's view: 'A military take-over and rule by officers never constitutes a revolution in Tropical Africa, but rather a limited modification of existing arrangements.'*

One obvious respect in which the military are better placed than civilians is their ability to adopt directly coercive measures to achieve their ends, be it the prevention of food hoarding or dealing with violent demonstrations. Indeed the events of 1963 in the Congo Republic and 1966 in Upper Volta indicate that hesitation to do this on the part of the civilian government allows the brief interval necessary for the army to identify itself with the rebels. Generally speaking military governments can run greater risks of confrontation with, for example, redundant workers than another type of administration: incidents in Ghana during the Nkrumah and Busia periods compared with similar situations under military government illustrate this point. Again this may simply be to say that in such circumstances the allegiance (and, therefore, the willingness to obey orders) of the security forces is less likely to be divided when they are serving a military government. It follows that, at any rate temporarily, a military régime has a better chance of implementing potentially unpopular austerity measures. On the other hand, a military government's willingness and ability to pursue unconciliatory policies may be carried too far; it is a fine point whether the federal military government in Nigeria

* A. R. Zolberg, 'Military Rule and Political Development in Tropical Africa: A Preliminary Report', in J. van Doorn (ed.), *Military Profession and Military Régimes*, The Hague, 1969.

displayed a lack of political finesse in allowing the country to get to the point where civil war became inevitable. It is, however, probable that only a military régime could, when the end of that war came, have had the confidence in its own strength to be generous and conciliatory to the defeated 'Biafrans'.

Comparisons of military–civilian behaviour in the field of foreign policy present even greater difficulty. The ability to perform effectively on the international stage is a useful qualification which helps to maintain or establish a political leader's position in the eyes of his own people. It may well be concluded that as with domestic policy so with foreign policy each case is *sui generis* – that, for instance, General Mobutu's external appearances and interventions have been largely ritual and concerned with the political and economic progress of his own country, while General Gowon's emergence as a dominant figure in the OAU was a product of the size and current dynamic development of his country. Colonel Acheampong in Ghana has played a lower key rôle externally than any of his predecessors since independence, while General Nimeiry has steered a careful course between satisfying his own and his neighbours' enthusiasm for the Palestinian cause in the Middle Eastern situation and maintaining a degree of non-involvement in militant Pan-Arab politics in order to give him a freer hand in relations with the West and the Communist worlds.

Military leaders with more than token military strength behind them have been and increasingly will be under some obligation to assert the African determination to be rid of white control over those parts of the continent sometimes referred to as 'the last outposts of colonialism'. They are in this respect in something of a dilemma, as General Gowon must be aware, for not only are these territories, with the exception of Guinea, geographically remote, but there seems to be little enthusiasm for allowing regular forces to become involved in training for guerilla warfare and insurrection. The implications of such involvement for military and civilian régimes alike are probably startlingly clear to the heads of state concerned.

The apparent organizational and other advantages of the military, such as discipline, administrative hierarchy, communications systems and an alleged reputation for patriotism and devotion to duty, have in Africa so far been more in evidence during the seizure of power than in the ultimate exercise of it. No overall generalization about the army as a national melting pot and symbol of unity can survive the litmus tests of the behaviour of the Nigerian army in 1966 and of the exploitation of the tribal divisions in the Ugandan force by Obote and Amin. All the apparent assets of the military can be matched by corresponding disadvantages or shown as not invariably producing the consequences which might be expected. Such a negative conclusion about military régimes in Africa does, however, relate to the comparatively small size of the armies concerned, their still rudimentary organization, the shallowness of their tradition and the corrosive effect of tribal and other factional divisions upon them. In all the cases described, with the possible exception of the Sudan, the army's institutional weakness has led to heavy reliance on the existing civilian bureaucracy and an inability to use military personnel to enforce the government's political will. In these circumstances an amalgam of styles of administration has proved inevitable.

Reduction of reliance on former politicians and civilian servants would clearly make for a more distinctively military type of administration. The appointment of army officers as regional commissioners or provincial governors has been common form, but it is a moot point whether any significant changes then result at lower levels in the administration. In this respect General Mobutu's shuffling of civil servants so that they served outside their native regions may have had at least some temporary effect on the character of the administration, such as might have been achieved by a larger-scale infusion of military.

It is certainly apparent, as evidenced by the first military régime in Ghana, that the ruling group's concern with its own legitimacy and with the nature of a successor government tends to undermine and diminish its involvement in the real substance of the country's problems. The result there was a classic, and in many senses, typical case of a military-police junta resorting perforce to rule through civilian administrators and institutions and continuing to use all the former channels of popular persuasion and influence, including the nuclei of reconstituted political parties which had been formally banned.

The positive achievements of governments with army officers at their head, duly noted in the cases of Ghana, Nigeria, Zaïre and the Sudan, are almost inevitably short-term: while they have not proved less competent or necessarily less just than civilians in their countries, they have certainly shown little propensity for lifting the level of political culture in Africa or facilitating radical social change. Land ownership, for example, remains in both Nigeria and the Sudan an obstacle to serious agricultural progress. The likely continuance and recurrence of military governments will certainly sharpen the political skills of the military at the expense of the evolution of a civilian political culture within which the means of coercion would be subordinate.

The prime factor tending to absorb the military into what might be optimistically termed the mainstream of African political development has been the absence on their part of any clear-cut political objectives. As has been said, in particular with regard to the Ghanaian situation in 1966-9, the soldiers were not only without ideological inspiration but failed to appreciate that political action in practice consists of a choice between imperfect alternatives. The likelihood in these circumstances is that where there is any political tradition at all the military will be gradually assimilated to it rather than the other way round.

Short Bibliography

Afrifa, A. A., *The Ghana Coup, February 24th 1966*, London, 1966.

Akiwowo, A., 'The Performance of the Nigerian Military Government from 1966 to 1970', in M. Janowitz and J. van Doorn (ed.), *On Military Intervention*, Rotterdam, 1971.

Bebler, Anton, *Military Rule in Africa: Dahomey, Ghana, Sierra Leone and Mali*, New York, 1973.

Bienen, Henry (ed.), *The Military Intervenes: Case Studies in Political Development*, New York, 1968.

Decalo, Samuel, 'Military Coups and Military Régimes in Africa', in *Journal of Modern African Studies*, Vol. 11, No. 1, 1973.

——, 'The Politics of Instability in Dahomey', in *Génève-Afrique*, No. 2, 1968.

Finer, S. E., *The Man on Horseback: the Rôle of the Military in Politics*, London, 1962.

First, Ruth, *The Barrel of a Gun*, London, 1970.

——, 'Uganda: the latest *coup d'état* in Africa', in *World Today*, March 1971.

Grundy, Kenneth, W., 'The Negative Image of Africa's Military', in *Review of Politics*, Vol. 30, No. 4, 1968.

Gutteridge, William F., *Armed Forces in New States*, London, 1962.

——, *Military Institutions and Power in the New States*, London, 1965.

——, *The Military in African Politics*, London, 1969.

—— (with Richard Booth), *The Armed Forces of African States 1970*, Adelphi Paper No. 67, Institute for Strategic Studies, 1970.

——, 'A Commonwealth Military Culture?', in *The Round Table*, July 1970.

——, 'Foreign Military Assistance and Political Attitudes in Developing African Countries', in *University of Sussex Institute of Development Studies Bulletin*, Vol. 4, No. 4, September 1972.

Huntington, Samuel P., *Political Order in Changing Societies*, New Haven, Conn., and London, 1968.

Janowitz, Morris, *The Military in the Political Development of New Nations*, Chicago, Ill., and London, 1964.

Kirk-Greene, A. H. M., *Crisis and Conflict in Nigeria 1966–1970*, Vols. I and II, London, 1971.

Lee, J. M., *African Armies and Civil Order*, London, 1969.

Lefever, Ernest, *Spear and Scepter*. The Brookings Institution, Washington, 1970.

Listowel, Judith, *Amin*, London and Dublin, 1973.

Luckham, A. R., *The Nigerian Military*, London, 1971.

——, 'Institutional Transfer and Breakdown in a New Nation: The Nigerian Military', in *Administrative Science Quarterly*, 1971.

Miners, N. J., *The Nigerian Army 1956–66*, London, 1971.

Nelkin, Dorothy, 'The Economic and Social Setting of Military Takeovers in Africa', in *Journal of Asian and African Studies*, Vol. II, Nos 3–4, 1967.

Nkrumah, Kwame, *Dark Days in Ghana*, London, 1968.

Nordlinger, Eric A., 'Soldiers in Mufti: the Impact of Military Rule upon Economic and Social Change in the Non-Western States', in *American Political Science Review*, Vol. 64, 1970.

Ocran, A., *A Myth is Broken: An Account of the Ghana Coup d'Etat*, London, 1968.

Panter-Brick, S. K. (ed.), *Nigerian Politics and Military Rule*, London, 1970.

Pinkney, Robert, *Ghana under Military Rule 1966–1969*, London, 1972.

——, 'The Theory and Practice of Military Government', in *Political Studies*, Vol. XXI, No. 2, June 1973.

Price, R. M., 'A Theoretical Approach to Military Rule in New States: Reference Group Theory and the Ghanaian Case', in *World Politics*, April 1971.

——, 'Military Officers and Political Leadership: the Ghanaian Case', in *Comparative Politics*, April 1971.

Rustow, D. A., *A World of Nations 1967* – Chapter Six, 'Military Régimes'.

St Jorre, John de, *The Nigerian Civil War*, London, 1972.

Twaddle, Michael, 'The Amin Coup', in *Journal of Commonwealth Political Studies*, Vol. X, No. 2, July 1972.

——, 'Order and Disorder in Uganda', in *The World Today*, October 1973.

Welch, Claude E. Jr. (ed.), *Soldier and State in Africa*, Evanston, Ill., 1970.

Williame, Jean Claude, *Patrimonialism and Political Change in the Congo*, Stanford, Calif., 1972.

Zolberg, Aristide R., 'Military Rule and Political Development in Tropical Africa', in J. van Doorn (ed.), *Military Profession and Military Régimes*, The Hague, 1969.

——, 'The Military Decade in Africa', in *World Politics*, January 1973.

Index

Index

For Product Safety Concerns and Information please contact our EU
representative GPSR@taylorandfrancis.com
Taylor & Francis Verlag GmbH, Kaufingerstraße 24, 80331 München, Germany

www.ingramcontent.com/pod-product-compliance
Lightning Source LLC
Chambersburg PA
CBHW050441280326
41932CB00013BA/2201